Romans: A Model for Bible Study Methods

Romans: A Model for Bible Study Methods

by
Lloyd M. Perry and Calvin B. Hanson

MOODY PRESS
CHICAGO

Library of Congress Cataloging in Publication Data

Perry, Lloyd Merle.
  Romans, a model for Bible study methods.

  Bibliography: p.
  1. Bible. N.T. Romans—Study. I. Hanson, Calvin B. II. Title.
BS2665.5.P47   227'.106   82-6281
ISBN 0-8024-7374-1   AACR2

Printed in the United States of America

Contents

Foreword

Never underestimate the impact of Paul's epistle to the Romans.

It was a text from Romans that brought spiritual light to the heart of Martin Luther, and the result was that mighty movement we call the Reformation.

It was while someone was reading aloud the preface to Luther's commentary on Romans that defeated John Wesley felt his heart "strangely warmed." The consequence of that little meeting in Aldersgate Street was the great Wesleyan Revival which, according to more than one historian, helped to save England from the same tragedies that befell France.

It was through the teaching of Romans by Robert Haldane in his rooms in Geneva, Switzerland, that a deep revival came, not only to the church in Switzerland, but also in France. Out of that ministry came Merle D'Aubigné, the church historian; Frederic Monod, leading founder of the Free churches in France; and Louis Gaussen, whose book *Theopneustia* is still a classic on biblical inspiration.

Evangelism; reformation; revival: certainly these are spiritual needs that must be met if the church today is going to make any kind of impact on our godless world. The epistle to the Romans gives us what we need.

The commentaries on Romans are legion. Why, then, another one?

Because this particular approach to Romans is unique. The authors bring to the study of Romans many years of practical experience in ministry as well as academic competence in exegesis and exposition of the Word. This is no ivory-tower study; it was hammered out in the marketplace of ministry where people hurt and only God's Word can help.

I am amazed at the vast amount of useful material in these pages. The seasoned student as well as the beginning pastor or teacher will find plenty of help in this book. However, I appreciate the fact that the authors not only help the reader, but they also show him how to help himself! Years of experience in the college and seminary classroom have taught these two men how to make Bible study a living experience instead of a dead responsibility.

Competent scholarship, practical help, spiritual warmth, and pastoral insight are all blended in this book, and you and I are the ones who benefit. I trust that this volume will be read and used by many, for each new generation needs to redig the old wells and drink deeply of the spiritual truths of God's Word.

WARREN W. WIERSBE

Introduction

With all the books on Romans presently reposing on library shelves and the constant flood of new volumes designed to furnish fresh insights into the apostle Paul's most profound letter, what necessity, or even justification, can there be for this present volume?

Perhaps the outstanding virtue of this book will prove to be its modest, yet urgent, down-to-earth intent—namely, to provide a provocative and practical study guide that may be used either by the individual as he works his way through the epistle on his own or by various Bible study groups. It is also the authors' desire that lay leaders and pastors without the benefit of tools and skills to work with the original text will find the volume helpful.

The reader will find a minimum of originality in terms of content, but it is hoped he will note a maximum of design in terms of form and purpose. The overriding intent throughout has been to provide in readily accessible form material that will stimulate the mind, warm the heart, and enable one to share with others the content of this New Testament book, which serves as a key to unlock the entire treasury of Scripture.

Three main approaches are taken to the text. First, the reader is asked to use the "telescope" to stand back and view from a distance the grand vistas of its content. Then, the "microscope" is used for smaller segments, and even individual words are examined minutely. Finally, there is the use of the "stethoscope," whereby the book is studied to provide nourishment for the soul and encouragement for the heart.

Paul's epistle to the Romans is commonly regarded to be the most his intended missionary trip to Spain and to solicit help for that venture (Rom. 15:23-24).

Paul's espistle to the Romans is commonly regarded to be the most complete and logical presentation of Christian truth in the entire New Testament. For centuries it has been regarded as the great defense of the faith.

Chrysostom had this epistle read to him once a week. Luther considered it the chief book of the New Testament. Melanchthon copied it twice with his own hand in order to know it thoroughly, and it was the book he lectured on most frequently.

Many testify to the influence of this epistle in their personal lives. Augustine was converted through reading Romans. Martin Luther launched the Reformation on Romans 1:17, "The just shall live by faith" (KJV).* John Wesley, founder of the Methodist church, was converted while listening to someone read from Luther's commentary on Romans.

If a Bible student wishes to master any one book of the Bible, let it be Romans. An understanding of this book is a key to unlocking the entire Word of God. Luther said, "This letter is the principal part of the New Testament and the purest gospel, which surely deserves the honour that a Christian man should not merely know it off by heart word for word, but that he should be occupied with it daily as the daily bread of the soul. For it can never be read too often and too well. And the more it is used the more delicious it becomes and the better it tastes."[1]

ROMANS IN RELATION TO OTHER NEW TESTAMENT EPISTLES

The letter to the Romans is unique among the New Testament letters in that it is more like a treatise and less like a personal letter than any other, save the epistle to the Hebrews. In writing to the saints at Rome whom he had not seen, Paul set forth truths in a well thought out and carefully organized way, whereas in his other letters he spoke of the same truths in a particularized way as need arose out of the specific circumstances. Consequently, we find in Romans the great themes of Paul's message and theology as never before coherently discussed in depth, breadth, and carefully considered manner. We read of the wrath and justice of God, justification by faith and by works, Adam and Christ, baptism and the new life, flesh and spirit, Israel's lack of faith and her final deliverance.

Justification by faith alone, the main theme of Romans, has already been treated by Paul in his letter to the Galatians, but now it is discussed extensively in chapter 4 against the backdrop of the depravity and misery of all men so clearly depicted in chapters 1 through 3.

In the same way, Romans 5:1-11, which speaks of God's act of reconciliation in Christ, seems to echo 2 Corinthians 5:17. An even clearer example is the way Paul's teaching about the antithetical typology of Adam and Christ in Romans 5:12-21 appears in 1 Corinthians 15:21, 45. In a similar vein, the thought that the law came to increase trespasses is developed with some fullness in Romans,

---

*King James Version.

along with themes such as death in Christ, life in the Spirit, and the freedom of God's children, which are simply stated or alluded to in earlier letters.

Romans 14 and 15 deal with the same subject matter as 1 Corinthians 8-10—the danger of using one's faith without consideration for one's brother. The Corinthian passage clearly reflects the peculiar situation in Corinth, whereas the Romans passage deals with the principle.

It may be helpful to divide the nine church epistles (omitting the personal or pastoral epistles) into three groups: those written first (1 and 2 Thessalonians); the middle group (Romans, 1 and 2 Corinthians, and Galatians); and the later epistles (Ephesians, Philippians, and Colossians). The epistle to the Romans, belonging to the second group of the Pauline epistles, was written about A.D. 55. Both Galatians and Romans were written in Corinth while Paul was there as a guest of Gaius who helped him to the leisure and the conveniences so necessary to the meditation and composition of two such epistles.

Romans is placed as the first epistle in the New Testament. The order of the New Testament letters follows the order given in 2 Timothy 3:16:

Doctrine—Romans (the great doctrinal book of the New Testament)
Reproof—1 and 2 Corinthians (where Paul reproves sin)
Correction—Galatians (where Paul corrects false teaching)
Instruction in Righteousness—Ephesians, and following (where Paul teaches holy living based on Christian doctrine).

It is significant that in our New Testament, Romans stands first among the epistles even though it was by no means the first to be written. J. Sidlow Baxter notes that each of Paul's letters has a distinctive emphasis and that each stands in relation to the others with Romans as the foundation:

Romans	The gospel and its message
1 Corinthians	The gospel and its ministry
2 Corinthians	The gospel and its ministers
Galatians	The gospel and its mutilators
Ephesians	The gospel and the heavenlies
Philippians	The gospel and the earthlies
Colossians	The gospel and the philosophies
1 Thessalonians	The gospel and the church's future
2 Thessalonians	The gospel and the Antichrist.[2]

Again, the same author locates each of the letters of Paul with a particular relation to Christology:

Romans	In Christ—justification
1 Corinthians	In Christ—sanctification
2 Corinthians	In Christ—consolation
Galatians	In Christ—liberation
Ephesians	In Christ—exaltation
Philippians	In Christ—exultation
Colossians	In Christ—completion
1 Thessalonians	In Christ—translation
2 Thessalonians	In Christ—compensation.[3]

The words which Mr. Baxter selects as key words of the various letters likewise illustrate the relationship which is maintained between the epistles:

Romans—righteousness
1 Corinthians—wisdom
2 Corinthians—comfort
Galatians—faith
Ephesians—blessed
Philippians—gain
Colossians—filled
1 Thessalonians—working
2 Thessalonians—waiting.[4]

THE ROMAN CHURCH

Paul wrote this epistle to the Christians in Rome. Although we may refer to the "church" at Rome, Paul does not address his letter to "the church at Rome," but rather "to all that be at Rome" (Rom. 1:7). In chapter 16 it becomes clear that there are different groups of believers (house churches) rather than one local assembly (vv. 5, 10-11, 14-15).

As far as we know, none of Paul's immediate associates in missionary labors had preceded him to Rome to found the church under his immediate direction and delegated authority. Although he did come to Rome later, he had nothing to do with the founding of the church. If neither Paul nor Peter, nor any other of the apostles or more prominent evangelists or missionaries can claim the honor of laying the foundation of the Christian church at Rome, how did the church come into being? We do not know, and are left to conjecture at this point.

Acts 2:10 does indicate that there were people from Rome in Jerusalem during Pentecost. We also know that Priscilla and Aquila were Roman Jews who knew the gospel. Note that the names in chapter 16 are largely Gentile, indicating that Gentile Christians from other cities had gravitated to Rome and carried the gospel with them. These were probably converts of Paul from other churches. Rome was the great center of the world in that day. It was not unlikely that thousands of pilgrims made their way over Roman highways to the Imperial City every year.

Romans 1:14-15, 11:13, and 15:14-16 all indicate that the majority of the believers who received the letter were Gentiles. There was also a Jewish element in the Christian community, as well as many Gentiles who were Jewish proselytes.

In spite of the fact that in the salutation Paul numbers the Romans among the Gentiles for whom he had been given the grace of apostleship (1:5-7), a large part of the epistle would be of chief interest to the Jews since it discusses the value of the Mosaic law and the dealings of God with the chosen people of Israel.

Both Jews and Gentiles, then, are in the church, and Paul addresses now one and now the other in the course of the epistle. There is no way of determining the exact proportion of those two classes, but the prevailing tendency at the present time is to conclude that the church was a Gentile church with a large and influential Jewish minority.

In Paul's day, the makeup of the church mirrored that of the city as a whole, and there were only fifty or sixty thousand Jews among them. The slaves outnumbered the freemen two or three to one.

Occasion of Writing

What motivated Paul to write this letter? He may have wanted to warn and teach the Christians at Rome lest false teachers arrive there before him and upset his plans. In Romans 3:8 Paul mentioned some false accusations certain men had made about him. The reasons, then, for the letter may be summarized as follows:

1. *To prepare* the Christians for his planned visit, and to explain why he had not visited them sooner (1:8-15, 15:23-29)
2. *To instruct* them in the basic doctrines of the Christian faith lest false teachers upset them
3. *To explain* the relationship between Israel and the church, lest the Judaizers lead them astray with their doctrines, and the Gentiles fail to appreciate their indebtedness to Israel
4. *To teach* the Christians their duties to one another and to the state
5. *To answer* any slander they may have heard about Paul (3:8).

The Heart of the Epistle

The Greeks sought after wisdom, and when Paul wrote letters to the Corinthians and to the Ephesians he laid great emphasis upon the acquisition of the true wisdom. Macknight calls it "a writing, which, for sublimity and truth of sentiment, for brevity and strength of expression, for regularity in its structure, but above all, for the unspeakable importance of the discoveries which it contains, stands unrivalled by any mere human composition, and as far exceeds the most celebrated productions of the learned Greeks and Romans, as the shining of the sun exceedeth the twinkling of the stars."[5]

Rome was not seeking wisdom so much as the universal recognition of law and order. Her mission was to establish justice throughout the length and the breadth of the earth. That may account for the fact that in writing this theological treatise for the Romans, Paul chose to give it a legal, forensic framework throughout.

In the term, "the righteousness of God" (1:17), the very foundational thought of the epistle to the Romans is encompassed. Here, in verse 17, Paul states the theme for his letter: "The righteousness of God is revealed from faith to faith; as it is written, 'But the righteous man shall live by faith.' " As the epistle proceeds it amplifies and clarifies the contents of this "righteousness of God." It includes the consequences for the Christian life of the new righteousness of God, which was revealed through Christ and is shared by everyone who believes in Him.

Every doctrine of the epistle is shown to have Old Testament authority behind it. There are more than fifty quotations from the Old Testament in these sixteen chapters—more than in all the other Pauline epistles put together. The phrase, "as it is written," occurs fourteen times as Paul, in this unique epistle, draws on the Old Testament Scriptures as background and foundation for his "Magna Carta" of the Christian faith.

Notes

1. Frederick L. Godet, *Commentary on the Epistle to the Romans* (Grand Rapids: Zondervan, 1956), p. ix.
2. J. Sidlow Baxter, *Explore the Book* (London: Marshall, Morgan & Scott, 1955), 6:64.
3. Ibid.
4. Ibid.
5. William S. Plumer, *Commentary on Romans* (Grand Rapids: Kregel, 1971), p. 30.

Part I

Using a "Telescope" to Survey the Epistle

Romans, among the epistles of the *New Testament*, stands out like an imposing Cathedral. Its symmetry of form, its logically developed structure, its evidence of plan and design, its wide sweep of thought, its sublimity and grandeur of revelation, all combine to make it one of the loveliest edifices of truth in existence.[1]

William G. Coltman

1

General Bible Study Methods

A serious study of the Bible requires concentration of the mind upon a specific passage. It involves giving careful consideration to words and phrases. The best available tools of biblical scholarship must be used in an honest attempt to learn as precisely as possible what the writer intended to communicate in the historical situation within which he wrote.

INDUCTIVE METHOD

The inductive method of Bible study is scientific in approach. It is the logic of discovery, whereas deduction is the logic of proof. Inductive Bible study involves four processes:

1. Observation (What does it say?)
2. Interpretation (What does it mean?)
3. Application (How does it relate to me?)
4. Communication (How do I give it to others?)

The inductive method places the emphasis on the process of reasoning or drawing conclusions from particular cases.

The Word of God must be given careful attention. It must be interpreted in full harmony with its literal, historical, and grammatical meaning. Full attention must be given to the inspired writer's purpose. When the student is face to face with the minute parts of Scripture, he must seek to know the intent of that Scripture in its context.

Robert A. Traina emphasizes the fact that the student should give special attention to the connectives within a passage. The following types of connectives are found in the New Testament:

1. Temporal or chronological connective:
   "After" (Rev. 11:11)

17

2. Local or geographical connective:
"Where" (Heb. 6:20)
3. Logical connectives:
Reason—"Because" (Rom. 1:25)
          "For" (Rom. 1:11)
Result—"Therefore" (1 Cor. 10:12)
Contrast—"Nevertheless" (1 Cor. 10:5)
4. Emphatic connective:
"Only" (1 Cor. 8:9).[2]

Traina also suggests that special attention be given to the structural relations between paragraphs and sections of the book. Out of his more extended list, we have selected five:

1. *Comparison*—the association of like things
2. *Contrast*—the association of opposites
3. *Repetition*—the reiteration of the same terms, phrases, and clauses
4. *Climax*—the arrangement of material in such a way as to progress from the lesser to the greater and ultimately to the greatest
5. *Causation and substantiation*—the progression from cause to effect and from effect to cause.[3]

SYNTHESIS

Synthesis is the "putting together of a book" or the consideration of it as a whole. This is the direct opposite of analysis, which attempts to partition a book into small units of study for the purpose of detailed investigation. With induction, conclusions are drawn on the basis of detailed observation; in synthesis, general impressions are gained by means of less detailed investigation, and the ramifications of those main ideas are not followed out in detail.[4]

ANALYSIS

Analysis is a detailed study of a book in order to ascertain its message in all its ramifications. It is the direct opposite of synthesis, which attempts to look at the book as a whole and to determine its message in general. In the development of this method, there must first be grammatical analysis, in which a study is made paragraph by paragraph. Determine the principal sentences and note the grouping around them of subordinate sentences and clauses, and their interrelationships. The analytical method begins with a grammatical diagram of the text, followed by a careful outline based on the diagram, and concludes with various observations on the message set forth.[5]

BIOGRAPHICAL METHOD

The biographical method may be studied factually us biographical narrative, homiletically as narrative or character exposition, and polemically or apologetically as biographical argument. In the biographical narrative, the aim is simply to learn the biographical facts concerning a biblical personality, as those details are revealed either in a single book or in all of Scripture. Some of the points to consider in a character's life include: 1) birth and early life; 2) conversion experience and call to a specific task; 3) ministry for the Lord; 4) character evaluation; 5) relationships with others; 6) death and comments about it; and 7) reasons for the inclusion of these facts in the text.[6]

THEOLOGICAL METHOD

The theological method may be defined as the process of searching through an individual book or the Bible as a whole to collect, compare, and organize doctrinal statements and assumptions.[7]

DEVOTIONAL METHOD

The devotional method may be effectively executed by means of a careful study of words, verses, paragraphs, chapters, books, Bible characters, and Christ in a given portion. In a survey course on the Bible one should include name, authorship, date, occasion, destination, key verse, literary style, outline and survey of contents, important chapters, special problems, canonicity, interpretation, the Christological element, and relationship to other Bible books.[8]

ADDITIONAL SUGGESTIONS

Additional suggestions are presented by Lawrence Richards. This is not Richards's complete list, but it includes items especially helpful in discovering the content of a passage.

Readings:
1. Read different interpretations of the passage to be studied.
2. Read parallel accounts in Scripture.
3. Read various versions.
4. Read looking for relationships (why? where? when? which? how?).

Projects:
1. Construct charts and graphs.
2. Diagram a passage of Scripture.
3. Prepare a research paper on a topic.
4. Write up a subject as a newspaper article.

Interviews and Surveys:
1. Interview resource individuals on the subject.
2. Interview "man on the street" for his opinion.
3. Prepare and distribute a questionnaire.
4. Make a list of problems people have with this subject.[9]

In reading a passage one should note carefully every verse that raises a question in one's mind, tells something about the person of God, pictures the thinking and actions of God's people, or seems to have parallels in modern life.[10]

The key to profitable Bible study is the addition of application to the exposition. The student should isolate the key thoughts, summarize those thoughts, and then draw some generalizations as to how they might apply to daily living.

The process of applying discovered biblical truth involves at least four steps according to Lawrence Richards in his *Creative Bible Study*.[11] First, derive from the passage of Scripture a principle that has relevance to daily living. The second step is to determine areas of life to which that principle might apply. In the third step one lists areas most relevant to personal needs. The last step sets forth the ways in which the applications can be made during the forthcoming week. Richards lists those steps as generalization, varied application, personalization, and determination.

NOTES

1. William G. Coltman, *The Cathedral of Christian Truth: Studies in Romans* (Findlay, Oh.: Fundamental Truth Publishers, 1943), Foreword.
2. Robert A. Traina, *Methodical Bible Study* (New York: Ganis and Harris, 1952), pp. 41-43.
3. Ibid., pp. 50-52.
4. Howard F. Vos, *Effective Bible Study* (Grand Rapids: Zondervan, 1956), p. 25.
5. Ibid., pp. 33-34.
6. Ibid., pp. 47-48.
7. Ibid., p. 74.
8. Ibid., pp. 173, 194.
9. Lawrence O. Richards, *Creative Bible Teaching* (Chicago: Moody, 1970), pp. 244-47.
10. Ibid., p. 249.
11. Lawrence O. Richards, *Creative Bible Study* (Grand Rapids: Zondervan, 1979), p. 164.

Probably this epistle should be regarded as the supreme master-piece of the great apostle. It is a marvel of intellectual acumen, of logical power, and of spiritual insight. However, it was first intended, not for the philosophers of the Imperial City, not for the savants of the schools, nor for the circle of Caesar's household, but for the members of an infant Christian church, composed largely of slaves and freedmen, recently delivered from a degrading heathenism and from the bondage of pagan superstitions. Therefore, in spite of its depth and its difficulties, it has been bringing light and strength to persons of widely differing degrees of intelligence through all the succeeding centuries. To none has its guidance been more grateful than to those troubled by the problems and perplexities of modern thought; for the gospel of Christ, which it sets forth, is still the sweetest music ever heard upon earth, the most powerful message proclaimed among men, the most precious treasure entrusted to the people of God.[1]

Charles R. Erdman

2

Personal Bible Study Projects
in Romans

1. Read Romans at one sitting. If you cannot do this, read chapters
   1-11, and at another sitting chapters 12-16. Or, read chapters 1-8,
   then chapters 9-16. In your first reading of Romans be alert to
   historical references and allusions that shed light on the circumstances under which Paul wrote the book. If possible, do your
   reading in a translation which you have not used before, or at
   least in a translation which employs modern English. An accurate, readable rendering is *The New American Standard Bible*,
   published by Moody Press.
2. After several overall readings, give an original title to each chapter, using the same criteria as above. These are more difficult
   because now you have to combine more ideas in a few words.
3. After several readings of individual chapters, give an original
   title to each paragraph. Good titles are brief—no more than
   three or four words; memorable—serve as mental hooks to recall
   the main idea(s) of the paragraph; and original—the product of
   your own mental mill.
4. In Romans 1:1-17, record *everything* this passage says about
   Paul, Christ, and the gospel.
5. Using a concordance, check the references to Rome in this epistle and in the book of Acts.
6. In Romans 1:1-32, How is the wrath of God revealed from heaven?
   Can you find at least four ways? What can we learn about God
   from nature? Why are the heathen lost? How can God be righteous and allow that?
7. Read Romans 1:18—3:20, looking for references to the ideas of
   wrath, punishment, and judgment.
8. Read Luke's account of Paul's sermon preached in Athens (Acts
   17:22-31) and the account of the message preached at Lystra (Acts
   14:15-17). Is there anything in those sermons that is similar to the
   thought in Romans 1:18-32?

9. From Romans 2:17—3:8:
   List and explain all the privileges and advantages of having been a Jew.
   List and explain all of the sins of which the Jews were guilty.
   List as many life principles as you can derive from this passage. Those are timeless truths applicable to anyone anywhere.
10. Name four principles of divine judgment as stated in chapter 2.
11. Read Romans 3:21—5:21, watching for recurring words and phrases.
12. In 4:1-25, list and explain everything Abraham illustrated about justification—especially of its acquisition and the results of having it.
13. Why could not God justify the Jews in one way, and the Gentiles in another way?
14. Read Romans 5:1-11. List and explain the benefits of having justification.
15. Study every occurrence of the word "life" in Romans 5-8. (Use a concordance if you wish.) Write out in your own words the essential teaching of each passage.
16. What is the ground of the believer's joy according to Romans 5:11? Why?
17. Study Romans 5:12-21. Contrast the two Adams, using this passage only. Make a chart of all the differences given here.
18. What was the function of law when it was introduced?
19. Read Romans 6:1-14. From this entire chapter, list at least ten spiritual truths and how they apply to you personally.
20. Explain why objections are raised to justification by faith alone as opposed to justification by faith and works.
21. From Romans 7:7-25, list everything mentioned in the passage about the old and new natures and their significances.
22. What is the main teaching of Romans 7:14-24? Think carefully.
23. Read Romans 8:1-39. Chart the work of the Trinity in this chapter. On separate sheets of paper, list everything said about the Father, the Son, and the Holy Spirit and the significance of each entry.
24. Use a concordance to study the New Testament teachings about the Holy Spirit. Where are most of the references to the Holy Spirit clustered?
25. What is the believer's greatest source of joy and strength in sufferings according to Romans 8:17-27?
26. List the references to Israel and define Paul's uses of the term.

27. From Romans 10:1-21, find as many answers as possible to the following questions:
    Is there an example to follow (positive example)?
    Is there an error to avoid (negative example)?
    Is there a command to be obeyed (my responsibility)?
    Is there a promise to claim (God's responsibility)?
    Is there a sin to confess (my responsibility)?
28. What is meant by the words, "going about to establish their own righteousness" (KJV) in Romans 10:3? How did Israel attempt this?
29. Read Romans 11:1-36. What warnings are given in this chapter? What personal application does each have?
30. How does Paul use the word "mercy" in chapters 9, 10, and 11?
31. How was the Gentile tempted to boast over Israel? Why should he not do it?
32. List the guidelines in chapter 12 for effective ministry in the church, and compare them with the spiritual gifts in 1 Corinthians 12 and Ephesians 4.
33. What is the outstanding virtue (in your opinion) enjoined upon the believer in Romans 12?
34. From Romans 12:9-21, list as many personal applications of Paul's admonitions as possible.
35. List the fifteen characteristics of God's love found in 1 Corinthians 13:4-7. See if you can find all of them in Romans 12 and 13.
36. After studying Romans 13:1-6, What is your opinion of a Christian's going to war for his country?
37. In Romans 14:1—15:13, What principles does God give us to make decisions in those areas where Scripture is not specific?
38. Read Romans 16:1-27. Note what is said about each individual.
39. Name some characteristics of first-century church life that can be gleaned from chapter 16.

NOTE

1. Charles R. Erdman, *The Epistle of Paul to the Romans: An Exposition* (Philadelphia: Westminster, 1925), Foreword.

The Epistle to the Romans is therefore encyclopaedic in its structure; it is round and full, like the circle of Giotto, and contains all the elements of both natural and revealed religion. The human mind need not go outside of this Epistle, in order to know all religious truth.[1]

William G. T. Shedd

3

Comparative Bible Book Outlines

It is important for a Bible student to develop some proficiency in outlining Bible content. One or more of the following suggestions may prove helpful.

The starting point for the outlining process is to read the Bible book through several times. A short book such as James could be read each day for a month. At the end of that time the main theme of the book and several of its logical divisions would have emerged. In studying a large book such as Acts, the individual might divide the twenty-eight chapters into seven parts and read each segment of the chapters each day for a week. That would mean spending seven weeks on that one book, but at the end of that time the theme and segments would have emerged.

A book of the Bible could be outlined by noting the chapter themes and charting them. The Bible as it was originally written had no chapter and verse divisions. But in A.D. 1250 Cardinal Hugot introduced chapter divisions that form fairly satisfactory groupings of content. There are 1,189 chapters in the Bible. The themes of the sixteen chapters in the book of Romans should then be related to the dominant theme of the entire book.

There are several types of outlines. Those include, among others, the thematic, geographical, chronological, and biographical. Illustrations of the first three can be seen in *How to Search the Scriptures.* [2] The biographical highlights the outstanding people within a Bible book. It would be evident through such an outline of the book of Acts, for instance, that Peter had the preeminence in the first half of the book and that Paul had the preeminence in the latter portion.

There are occasions in which a key verse will provide a possible clue for a Bible book outline. That is evident in some of the outlines of the book of Revelation, which are based upon the three emphases in Revelation 1:19.

Two additional devices include noting repeated words and phrases, and changes in the type of content. The latter can be illustrated in the book of Job, where several messages are inserted in the narrative text.

The four outlines included in this section have unique features. The first one shows the development of a doctrinal theme within the book. The second also develops a doctrinal theme but adds additional doctrinal emphases. The third outline highlights the major divisions of the book in terms of major emphases such as doctrinal, dispensational, and practical. The fourth outline emphasizes the rhetorical device of alliteration, which is often used in outlining since it provides assistance in memorizing the content of the outline.

Outline showing development of a doctrinal theme within Romans.

OUTLINE: BOOK OF ROMANS

I. Introduction (1:1-17)
  A. The Preface of the Epistle (1:1-7)
    1. The salutation (1:1)
    2. The signification (1:2-7)
  B. The Personalities of the Epistle (1:8-13)
    1. The interest (1:8-10)
    2. The intent (1:11-13)
  C. The Purpose of the Epistle (1:14-17)
    1. The motive (1:14-15)
    2. The method (1:16-17)
II. The Lack of Righteousness (1:18—3:20)
  A. The Gentile world is proved guilty of sin (1:18—2:16)
    1. The revelation that God made of Himself (1:18-20)
    2. The stages of Gentile apostasy from God (1:21-23)
    3. The results of the Gentile apostasy (1:24-32)
    4. The principles of divine judgment (2:1-16)
  B. The Jewish world is guilty of sin (2:17—3:20)
    1. The law finds the Jewish world guilty of sin (2:17-29)
    2. The Old Testament Scriptures generally find the Jewish world guilty of sin (3:1-18)
    3. The final verdict—The world is guilty of sin before God, hence, the imperative need of righteousness (3:19-20)
III. The Provision of Righteousness (3:21-26)
  A. The righteousness defined (3:22)
  B. The righteousness attested (3:21)
  C. The righteousness offered (3:22)

      1. To all
      2. On faith
      3. Freely
      4. By grace
  D. The ground of righteousness (3:24)
  E. The purpose of the righteousness (3:26)
  F. The Author of the righteousness (3:25)
IV. The Appropriation of Righteousness (3:27—4:25)
  A. On faith in Christ (3:27—4:4)
  B. Not of works (4:5-8)
  C. Not of ordinances (4:9-12)
  D. Not of law (4:13-23)
  E. But through the death and resurrection of Christ (4:24-25)
V. The Realization of Righteousness (5:1—8:17)
  A. Deliverance from condemnation before God through the death of Christ (5:1-21)
  B. Deliverance from indwelling sin (6:1-12)
  C. Deliverance from the law (6:13—7:25)
  D. Deliverance from the flesh (or self life) through the Holy Spirit who comes from Christ (8:1-17)
VI. The Guarantee of Righteousness (8:18-39)
  A. Creation being kept for the children of God (8:18-25)
  B. The indwelling of the Holy Spirit (8:26-27)
  C. The eternal purpose of God (8:28-30)
  D. The death, resurrection, and exaltation of Christ (8:31-32, 34)
  E. The character of God (8:33)
  F. The one made righteous before God in the righteousness provided in Christ is made eternally safe (8:35-39)
VII. The Rejection of Righteousness (9:1—11:36)
  A. Notwithstanding the covenant blessings (9:1-5)
  B. Notwithstanding a holy natural descent (9:6-13)
  C. Notwithstanding the sovereignty of divine mercy (9:14-33)
  D. The rejection of God's righteousness on the part of the Jews; their own fault (10:1-21)
  E. But spiritual Israel is finding and receiving the righteousness of God (11:1-6)
  F. National Israel is judicially blinded and cannot even see the righteousness of God (11:7-12)
  G. Gentile Christians who have received the righteousness of God are warned (11:13-26)
  H. National Israel notwithstanding their past and present rejection of that righteousness shall in the future be saved through that righteousness (11:27-36)

VIII. The Practice of Righteousness (12:1—15:13)
    A. In Christian duties (12:1-21)
       1. In Christian consecration (12:1)
       2. In Christian transformation (12:2)
       3. In Christian service (12:3-8)
       4. In Christian fellowship (12:9-16)
       5. In Christian conduct in relation to those without (12:17-21)
    B. In civil duties (13:1-7)
    C. In social duties (13:8-14)
    D. In fraternal duties (14:1—15:13)
IX. Conclusion: Personal Matters (15:14—16:27)
    A. The apostle's ministry (15:14-22)
    B. His approaching journey (15:23-33)
    C. His commendatory note (16:1-16)
    D. His word of warning (16:17-18)
    E. His word of praise (16:19)
    F. His word of promise (16:20a)
    G. His benediction (16:20b)
    H. His salutation (16:21-24)
    I. His ascription of praise (16:25-27)

Outline showing doctrinal themes with additional doctrinal emphases.

THE EPISTLE OF PAUL TO THE ROMANS

Introduction—salutation	1:1-17
The author—Paul	1:1
The theme—"The gospel of God"	1:1
The readers—the saints at Rome	1:7-15
Key verses—Romans 1:16-17	
Key word—"righteousness"	
I. Righteousness Required—condemnation	1:18—3:20
A. The Gentile guilty	1:18—2:16
B. The Jew guilty	2:17—3:18
C. Final verdict—a guilty world	3:19-20
II. Righteousness Revealed—salvation	3:21—4:25
A. Redemption in Christ	
1. Without the law	
2. By grace	
3. Through faith	
4. Without works	3:21-31

B. Old Testament illustrations of redemption
   1. Abraham   4:1-5, 9-25
   2. David   4:6-8
III. Righteousness Received—justification   5:1-21
A. Our heritage in Christ   5:1-11
   1. Justification   5:1
   2. Peace   5:1
   3. Access   5:2
   4. Glory   5:2
   5. Hope   5:4-5
   6. Love   5:5, 8
   7. Joy   5:11
B. Our heritage in Adam   5:12-21
   1. Sin   5:12-15
   2. Death   5:16-17
   3. Judgment   5:18-21
IV. Righteousness Realized—sanctification   6:1—7:25
A. The believer to reckon himself
   1. Dead to sin
   2. Alive to the law
   3. Alive and yielded to Christ   6:1—7:25
B. The Holy Spirit operates in the
   life of the yielded believer   8:1-39
V. Righteousness Rejected—repudiation   9:1—11:36
A. Israel's past   9:1-33
B. Israel's present   10:1-21
C. Israel's future   11:1-36
VI. Righteousness Reproduced—consecration   12:1—15:7
(The will of God for the Christian)
The Christian's Responsibility
A. To God   12:1-2
B. To the body of Christ   12:3-16
C. To the world   12:17—13:14
D. To government   13:1-7
E. To "the one who is weak in faith"   14:1—15:7
Conclusion—benediction   15:8—16:27
   Praise   15:8-13
   Paul—the apostle to the Gentiles   15:14-21
   Personal greetings   15:22—16:23
   Benediction   16:20, 24-27

Outline showing major divisions in terms of major emphases.

ANALYSIS OF ROMANS

Prologue (1:1-17)
  1. Salutation (1:1-7)
  2. Introduction (1:8-15)
  3. Proposition (1:16-17)
I. DOCTRINAL—PHILOSOPHY OF SALVATION (1:18—8:39)
The righteousness of God in relation to sin and sins
  A. The Christian Message (1:18—5:21)
    (Propitiation and Foundation)
    Christ for Us—Key: 1:16-17
    1. Theme: Condemnation (1:18—3:20)
      a. The Gentiles under condemnation (1:18-32)
      b. The Jews under condemnation (2:1—3:8)
      c. The world under condemnation (3:9-20)
    2. Theme: Justification (3:21—5:11)
      a. The ground of justification—God's grace (3:21-26)
      b. The means of justification—our faith (3:27—4:25)
      c. The effects of justification—spiritual fruit (5:1-11)
  Supplementary (5:12-21)
Condemnation and justification traced to their historical
sources in Adam and Christ.
  B. The Christian Life (6:1—8:39)
    (Identification and Superstructure)
    Christ in Us—Key: 5:9-10
    1. Theme: Sanctification (6:1—8:11)
      a. The principle of holiness (6:1-11)
        (in death and resurrection with Christ)
      b. The practice of holiness (6:12—7:6)
        (in recognition of, and abandonment to, the new rela-
        tions)
      c. The preventive of holiness (7:7-25)
        (in the activity within—of sin and self)
      d. The power of holiness (8:1-11)
        (in the unhindered dominion of the Spirit of God)
    2. Theme: Glorification (8:12-30)
      a. The evidence of coming glory (12-17)
      b. The expectation of coming glory (18-27)
      c. The certainty of coming glory (28-30)
  Supplementary (8:31-39)

From condemnation to glorification; celebrated in a triumphant song.

II. DISPENSATIONAL—PHILOSOPHY OF HISTORY (9:1—11:36)
The righteousness of God in relation to the calling of Israel
   A. The Election of Israel—past (9:1-29)
   B. The Rejection of Israel—present (9:30—10:21)
   C. The Conversion of Israel—future (11:1-32)
      Doxology (11:33-36)

III. PRACTICAL—PHILOSOPHY OF CONDUCT (12:1—16:27)
The righteousness of God in relation to everyday life
   A. Paths of Duty (12:1—13:14)
      1. Religious (12:1-13)
      2. Social (12:14-21)
      3. Civil (13:1-14)
   B. Principles of Action (14:1—15:13)
      1. Christian liberty (14:1-12)
      2. Christian love (14:13-23)
      3. Christian unity (15:1-13)
   Epilogue (15:14—16:27)
      1. Purpose and plans (15:14-33)
      2. Greetings and warning (16:1-24)
      3. Ascription of praise (16:25-27)

Outline using rhetorical device of alliteration.

ROMANS: THE THEOLOGY OF THE GOSPEL

Prologue (1:1-17)
   I. The Principles of Christianity (1-8)
      A. The Question of Sin (1:18—3:20)
      B. The Question of Salvation (3:21—5:21)
      C. The Question of Sanctification (6:1—8:39)
  II. The Problem of Christianity (9-11)
      A. God's Past Dealings with Israel (9:1-33)
      B. God's Present Dealings with Israel (10:1-21)
      C. God's Promise Dealings with Israel (11:1-36)
 III. The Practice of Christianity (12-16)
      A. The Laws of Christian Life (12:1—13:7)
         1. The spiritual life of the Christian (12:1-13)
         2. The social life of the Christian (12:14-21)
         3. The secular life of the Christian (13:1-7)
      B. The Laws of Christian Love (13:8—16:24)

1. Love's conscience (13:8-14)
2. Love's considerations (14:1 — 15:3)
3. Love's convictions (15:4-13)
4. Love's concern (15:14-33)
5. Love's contacts (16:1-16)
6. Love's conquests (16:17-20)
7. Love's companionships (16:21-24)

Epilogue (16:25-27)

NOTES

1. William G. T. Shedd, *A Critical and Doctrinal Commentary of the Epistle of St. Paul to the Romans* (Minneapolis: Klock & Klock, 1978), Preface.
2. Lloyd M. Perry and Robert D. Culver, *How to Search the Scriptures* (Grand Rapids: Baker, 1967).

The Epistle to the Romans ought to be the manual of the theological student and clergyman, because it is in reality an inspired system of theology. The object of the writer was to give to the Roman congregation, and ultimately to Christendom, a complete statement of religious truth. It comprises natural religion, the gospel, and ethics; thus covering the whole field of religion and morals. [1]

William G. T. Shedd

4

Methods for Surveying a Bible Book

HOW TO DO BACKGROUND STUDY

The following list of suggestions and questions will serve as a guide for doing background study on a Bible book.

1. *Discover the main theme of the book.* This should be in the form of a title or phrase. Decide upon your own theme after having read the book, and then compare it with those given in books of Bible introduction.
2. *Learn what you can about the writer.* Look for reflections of the author's personality found in the book. List those, giving a chapter and verse reference for each.
3. *Where was the book written?* If possible, this should be determined through a reading of the book itself. Give the chapter and verse you use as a basis for your conclusion. If there is no indication within the book, then check a work on Bible introduction.
4. *When was the book written?* Give chapter and verse references from the book that indicate definite points of time. Locate the time of the writing of the book within the life span of the author.
5. *To whom was the book written?* Give a chapter and verse reference if there is internal evidence. Otherwise, check an outside source.
6. *What problems in their lives made the book necessary?* What emergency was the book designed to meet? Give evidences of this emergency found within the text, and elaborate by using material from at least one outside source.
7. *List by chapter and verse any peculiar or repeated terms.* When terms appear to be outstanding due to the number of times they are repeated, count them and record the number. Peculiar terms are those which attract your attention while reading and seem to be unique to a particular book.
8. *What does the book teach concerning the Godhead?* List the chapter and verse of each reference to the Father, the Son, and the Holy Spirit.

9. *What references may indicate major divisions in the structure of the book?* These may be in the form of repeated phrases, abrupt changes of subject, person, or rhetorical form.[2]

BACKGROUND STUDY OF THE BOOK OF ROMANS

1. *The main theme of the book.* Possible suggestions are:
   Righteousness through faith
   The epistle of faith
   The book of righteousness
   Justification by faith
   The logic of the Christian faith
   How can a man be just before God?
2. *Who was the human author?* Paul, the great apostle (1:1).
   He was a Hebrew, a native of Tarsus, and educated by Gamaliel in Jerusalem
   He was hindered from going to Rome (1:13)
   His ancestry (11:1)
   His going to Judea (15:31)
   His acquaintances (chap. 16).
3. *Where was the book written?* Corinth.
   It was written from Corinth while Paul was a guest of Gaius. Tertius was his scribe (16:22).
   The letter was taken to Rome by a wealthy widow named Phoebe, who went there on some personal business (16:1-2).
4. *When was the book written?* A.D. 55.
   It was written during the time of the Third Missionary Journey of Paul. The two letters to the Corinthians were written about the same time.
5. *To whom was the book written?* The Christians at Rome.
6. *What problems made the book necessary?*
   Charges had been laid against Paul's theology. It was uncertain as to how long his life would be spared. He felt constrained to leave a theological treatise that would clarify his own convictions and also serve as a doctrinal foundation for the believers. He endeavored to make plain to the minds of the readers the full gospel message as it is revealed by God in the person and sacrificial work of Jesus Christ.
7. *What are some of the peculiar or repeated terms?*
   Repeated terms: all (71), Christ (51), faith (62), flesh (20), impute (19), justification (18), law (73), righteousness (66), sin (60).

Peculiar terms: free gift (5:18), give account (14:12), grafted in (11:19), propitiation (3:25).

8. *What does the book teach concerning the Godhead?*
There are 150 references to God
There are 66 references to Christ
There are 5 references to the Holy Spirit
We have redemption in Christ (3:24)
We have peace with God through Christ (5:1)
Christ died for the ungodly (5:6)
We are saved by the blood of Christ (5:9)
The gift of God in Jesus Christ is eternal life (6:23)
There is no condemnation to those in Christ (8:1)
The love of God is in Christ Jesus (8:39)
God raised Jesus from the dead (10:9).

9. *What are some of the possible indicators of outline divisions?*
There appear to be thought transitions between:
1:17 and 1:18
8:39 and 9:1
11:36 and 12:1
15:13 and 15:14.

How to Do Content Study

The following steps will aid in studying the content of a Bible book.
1. Read the book through to find:
   • The main theme of the book
   • The key verses of the book.
2. Trace the development of the main theme in the light of:
   • The problems presented
   • The general tone of the book (argumentation, exhortation, instruction)
   • Types of reasoning employed
   • Unique expressions employed
   • Outstanding affirmations
   • Grammatical peculiarities.
3. Establish an outline. In doing this, take special note of possible hints given by the author, repeated phrases, abrupt changes of subject, persons, and rhetorical form. It is suggested that you follow the text by paragraphs.
4. Compare three outlines of the book to determine the thematic segments. Check three good books of Bible introduction for the

purpose of comparing their outlines. For example, note where each author suggests the first break for the introduction to the book. Use the unanimous or majority decision of those writers to determine the outstanding points of division within the outlines.

5. Compose a list of the most common thematic segments to cover the content of the book.
6. Apply one or both of the following study guides to thematic segments:

Study Guide One

(1) Suggest a theme for each thematic segment.
(2) Outline the contents of the passage.
(3) List the words and phrases that need definition.
(4) Show differences between the King James Version and one other version.

Study Guide Two

(1) *Who?* — personal. List and summarize the material in the passage pertaining to each character listed.
(2) *Where?* — locational. Locate geographically each place referred to; list important incidents that have taken place at each location.
(3) *When?* — temporal. Locate this passage as to time in light of the immediate context, and also in respect to the writer's life span.
(4) *What?* — definitive. Explain words needing definition. Establish a thematic analytical outline of the passage.
(5) *Why?* — rational. What was the purpose behind the presentation of this passage in the Bible?
(6) *Wherefore?* — implicational. List the conclusions gathered from the passage as they pertain to: (1) theology; and (2) daily experience.

7. Formulate a list of study projects that will lead you into further specific research within the book.[3]

HOW TO STUDY A BIBLE CHAPTER

The following questions will serve as a guide for studying Bible chapters.

1. *What is the theme of the chapter?* Read the chapter in its entirety in one sitting and put into a phrase what you consider to be the main thought of the chapter.

2. *Which is the key verse in the chapter?* Make your selection on the basis of the verse that has special appeal for you from the standpoint of practical and spiritual refreshment.
3. *What personages are mentioned? What information is included regarding each one mentioned?* Make a tabulated list of the people and information giving the reference for each.
4. *What commands should we obey?* List these in tabulated form, giving the reference for each.
5. *What promises should we claim?* List these in tabulated form, giving the reference for each.
6. *What lessons should we remember?* List these in tabulated form, giving the reference for each.
7. *Which words and phrases did you like best?* List these in tabulated form, giving the reference for each.
8. *Which words kept recurring throughout the chapter?* Count the number of times the words recurred and give a statement for each as to its meaning and pertinence to the general thought of the chapter.
9. *Which words were not clear as to their meaning?* List these giving chapter and verse and check the meaning in a concordance or Bible dictionary.
10. *What logical reason can you detect for the inclusion of this chapter in the Bible?* Note what would be missing from the general biblical account if this chapter had been omitted by divine decree.
11. *What errors of living should we avoid?* Be specific in your statement of each error, and give the reference for each.
12. *What does this chapter teach about God?* List each reference to the Father, the Son, and the Holy Spirit.[4]

CHAPTER STUDY OF ROMANS 5

1. Theme: God did a lot more good for man through Christ than Adam did harm through sin because reconciliation is received through faith in Christ (vv. 1, 6, 8, 11, 17).
2. Key verse: 5:8—"God demonstrates His own love for us, in that while we were yet sinners, Christ died for us."
   This assures me of God's love. When I feel I have given in and am in a pattern of sin, I remember that Christ loved me and died for me even when I was (am) a sinner. It helps me get over guilt and fear that accumulates with trying to "measure up" as a Christian and lets me relax and start again to abide (and obey) with Him.

3. Personages mentioned:
 Jesus Christ—died for the ungodly (us); many have been jus-
     tified through His blood and saved from God's
     wrath (entire chapter).
 Adam—was a pattern of the One (Jesus) to come.
     He sinned and thus brought condemnation and death
     (for all men). (vv. 12, 14-19)
 Moses—death reigned from Adam till his time (v. 14).

4. Commands to obey:
 None.

5. Promises to claim:
 We have peace because we have been justified by our faith in
  Jesus Christ (v. 1)
 Promise that suffering produces perseverance, which produces
  character, which produces hope in the glory of God (v. 3)
 Hope will not disappoint us (v. 5)
 We will be saved from God's wrath because we have been jus-
  tified by Christ's blood (v. 9)
 Those who receive God's grace and righteousness will reign in
  life through Jesus Christ (v. 17)
 We can be justified to have eternal life due to Christ's act of
  righteousness (v. 18)
 Promise that grace is greater than power of sin so that it reigns
  through righteousness to bring eternal life (vv. 20-21).

6. Lessons to remember:
 Sin reigns in death; grace reigns to bring eternal life (v. 21)
 The gift is not like the trespass (v. 15)
 It is rare that someone dies for a good person. But God's love is
  shown by Christ's having died for sinners (vv. 7-8).

7. Words and phrases I liked best:
 We have peace with God (v. 1)
 We rejoice in the hope of the glory of God (v. 2)
 Perseverance and character (v. 4)
 God has poured out His love into our hearts by the Holy Spirit
  (v. 5)
 The gift is not like the trespass (v. 15)
 The gift followed many trespasses and brought justification
  (v. 16)
 Grace increased all the more (v. 20).

8. Recurring words:
 Justified, faith, grace, reconcile/reconciliation, rejoice, righ-
  teous(ness), life, condemnation, hope, sin, ungodly, sinners,

enemies, trespass, death/died, law, command, gift.
9. If this chapter were missing . . .
The chapter explains in detail sin and its effects in contrast to justification through faith (how justification came about and what its effects and countereffects are). It helps us to really see in a clear way that it is a gift of grace that Christ should die for us as sinful people so that we could have peace with God and be reconciled to Him.
10. Errors of living to avoid:
Not rejoicing in suffering (v. 3)
Forgetting that God has poured his love into our hearts by the Holy Spirit. We shouldn't be dry of love if this is true (v. 5)
We should avoid sin (v. 12).

Questions:
1. What is the meaning of "justified" (v. 1)?
2. Why does verse 14 say that death reigned from Adam to Moses?
3. How does the "because" half of verse 5 relate to hope's not disappointing us?
4. What was Christ's act of righteousness (v. 18)? Why is His death on the cross as payment for our sin "righteous" rather than "merciful?" His righteousness was His resurrection. Why is that particularly "righteous?" His obedient life was righteousness. Why is it referred to as just one act?

How to Study a Bible Doctrine

The ultimate aim of Bible study is to understand its "doctrines" so that we may apply them to our lives. By doctrine we mean "that which is taught," the orderly statement of particular truths.

Some of the Bible Doctrines

Adoption	Christ	Election
Angels	Christ's Second	Eternal Life
Antichrist	Coming	Existence of God
Atonement	Church	Faith
Attributes of God	Covenants	Fall of Man
Backsliding	Conversion	Forgiveness
Baptism	Creation	Glorification
Blood	Death	Grace
(of sacrifices)	Demonology	Heaven
Character of Sin	Dispensations	Hell

Holiness	Mystical Union	Repentance
Holy Spirit	Origin of Man	Revelation
Immutability	Original Sin	Rewards
of God	Penitence	Righteousness
Inspiration	Perseverance	Salvation
Israel	of Saints	Sanctification
Judgment	Prayer	Satan
Justification	Predestination	Scriptures, the
Kingdom of God	Priestly Office	Separation
Knowledge of God	of Christ	Sin Offering
Last Things	Prophetic Office	Sovereignty
Law	of Christ	of God
Liberty	Providence	Temptation
Lord's Supper	Punishment	Trinity
Love	Reconciliation	Virgin Birth
Miracles	Regeneration	Works

The study of a doctrine as it appears in the entire Bible is beyond the ability of most beginning students. It is preferable for the new Christian to study a doctrine in one particular book. After reaching his conclusions from that book, he can then expand the study by going on to other books. Using the following steps should prove helpful in studying a Bible doctrine.

1. Collect all references to the doctrine. Trace those by the use of an analytical concordance or topical Bible.
2. Define the doctrine by comparing all Bible references, by using such extrabiblical helps as necessary, and by formulating a concise, clear statement of its meaning.
3. Relate the references to their immediate context and the total pattern of biblical truth. Study each reference in the light of its context and evaluate the presence of this doctrine within the total pattern of the biblical revelation, cataloging them according to the various aspects of the subject they present.
4. Apply the doctrine to personal experience. Is this a doctrine for believers or unbelievers? In what way must it be applied to the lives of those to whom it is addressed?
5. Summarize the doctrine. Write a paragraph or more stating your conclusions; that is, write a concise statement of its content and its importance.[5]

NOTES

1. William G. T. Shedd, *A Critical and Doctrinal Commentary on the Epistle of St. Paul to the Romans* (Minneapolis: Klock & Klock, 1978), Preface.
2. Lloyd M. Perry and Robert D. Culver, *How to Search the Scriptures* (Grand Rapids: Baker, copyright 1967), pp. 111-12. Used by permission.
3. Ibid., pp. 115-16.
4. Ibid., pp. 142-43.
5. Ibid., pp. 174-77.

Part II

Using a "Microscope" to Study the Content of the Epistle

The Epistle to the Romans is the first great work of Christian theology. From the time of Augustine it had immense influence on the thought of the West, not only theology but also in philosophy and even in politics, all through the Middle Ages. At the time of the Reformation its teaching provided the chief intellectual expression for the new spirit of religion. For us men of Western Christendom there is probably no other single writing so deeply imbedded in our heritage of thought.[1]

C. H. Dodd

5

Segment Study

We have gazed through the "telescope" to survey the broad sweep of the epistle to the Romans. We now set aside that instrument and take the "microscope" to begin the exciting discipline of examining minutely the terrain before us, bit by bit, verse by verse, and, at times, word by word.

If we believe, as we surely do, that the inspiration of the Scriptures extends to the very words in such a way that the human authors were infallibly guided by the Holy Spirit—even to the selection of individual words—then we owe to the text the most careful examination and the closest scrutiny of those words, which we do affirm to be the very words of the living God.

Our method in the segment study portion will be closely related to that followed by Newman and Nida in *A Translator's Handbook on Paul's Letter to the Romans*, a volume we commend to the reader who has a particular interest in this kind of study.

Taking the divine inspiration of the Bible seriously as we do, we must be concerned not only for the words themselves but for the nuances of grammar and syntax of the language in which the New Testament was written. Consequently, references to matters of Greek grammar such as voice and mood of the verb have been necessary. It is hoped that such references will be of genuine help to the reader in English and add rather than detract from the significance of comments on specific items.

ROMANS 1:1-7   PAUL AND HIS GOSPEL

1:1-7   The introductory sentence comprises the first seven verses of the letter and contains 126 words. In no other letter of Paul is the first sentence as long or so full of significance. With the exception of the epistle to the Hebrews, this could also be said of the entire New Testament. More important, this introductory sentence is unusually rich in theological content and in that respect serves admirably as an appetizer for the rich feast that is to come.

If the sentence is distinctive in theological content, it is certainly so in style and suggests that we ought to anticipate a carefully crafted letter (unusual for Paul). The first six words form a kind of double chiastic construction that can hardly be accidental. "Paul servant of Christ, of Jesus called apostle." The innermost terms correspond to one another as do the middle terms and the outer terms — apparently designed to catch one's eye.

Farrar says of this salutation, "It is the longest and most solemnly emphatic of those found in any of the Pauline epistles. . . . In one grand single sentence, of which the unity is not lost in spite of digressions, amplifications and parentheses, he tells the Roman Christians of his solemn setting apart, by grace, to the apostolate; of the object and universality of that apostolate; of the truth that the gospel is no daring novelty, but the preordained fulfillment of a dispensation prophesied in Scripture; of Christ's descent from David according to the flesh, and of his establishment with power as the Son of God according to the spirit of holiness by the resurrection from the dead."[2]

1:1a   "Paul, a *bond-servant* of Christ Jesus." This is more literally, "slave of Jesus Christ." This is the only time that Paul so designates himself in the opening sentence of a letter to a church. However, in writing to Titus, an individual, he does use the same term. It is interesting that of all the churches to whom Paul writes, he uses this term only when writing to the church in the capital of the empire whose emperor was called "Lord." The phrase, "slave or servant (Gr. *doulos*) of the emperor" occurs frequently in inscriptions.

1:1b   "*Set apart* for the gospel of God." The word literally means to "mark off by boundaries," and so, "to set apart." The form of the participle suggests that Paul has by conscious act and specific commitment been so set apart and that the results of that act continually determine his way of life.

       "Set apart for the gospel *of God.*" The letter begins with a reference to "the gospel *of God*" and concludes with a reference to "*my* gospel" (16:25).

1:1   "*Bond-servant.*" Literally "slave" from a word that means "to bind."

       "*Gospel.*" "Good news." This is a translation of the New

Testament word from which we get "evangelism."

Paul characterizes himself not only as slave but as an *apostle*. This term refers to the twelve who were commissioned by our Lord during his earthly ministry and is also used in a broader sense to include others (Acts 14:4-14; Rom. 16:7; 1 Cor. 12:28; Eph. 4:11). Although Paul is not one of the twelve, he considers his apostleship to be equal with theirs (1 Cor. 9:1-2) and his gospel fully authoritative (Gal. 1:11-12).

1:2   The prophet was the person who spoke to men the message of God, not merely one who foretold the future (Moses, David, and Solomon, along with others, are called prophets). Here, the emphasis is on the fact that what God promised through the *prophets* has come true.

1:4   "Who through the Spirit of holiness *was declared* with power to be the Son of God." This is the same verb translated "set apart" and referred to in the first comment on 1:1b.

"*Declared.*" Better "designated" (marked out by a sure sign).

"*Jesus.*" The personal name (Matt. 1:21).

"*Christ.*" The official name, "Anointed" (John 1:41, 45).

"*Lord.*" The family name (John 13:13-14).

1:5   "*Grace.*" Unmerited favor.

"*Among all the Gentiles*" refers to peoples from all nations. Some take the Greek word in the more restrictive sense, That is, "pagan" (JB)* or "heathen" (Goodspeed).

1:7   "Called *as* saints." The word in italics is inserted and misleading. We are called saints. That is central to the epistle. Because the righteousness of Christ is reckoned ours, we are named saints.

"*Saints.*" The word means "holy ones" or "set-apart ones." This is God's designation of a believer.

"*Beloved of God*" translates the Greek genitive case. The Greek word "beloved" is used throughout the New Testament to indicate strong endearment, including that of the Father for the Son (Matt. 3:17; 17:5).

"*Grace*" and "*peace*" is a frequent combination in early Christian greetings and is the standard salutation in all of Paul's letters. It combines the Christian concept "grace" with the Jewish "peace." "Grace" expresses God's love and mercy toward undeserving people. "Peace" sums up all the benefits of God's gracious act.

Jerusalem Bible

Translations and Interpretations for Consideration

1:4   "Installed as Son of God with power by the Spirit of holiness when he was raised from the dead" (Moffatt).*
       "Who was physically descended from David, and decisively declared Son of God in his holiness of spirit, by being raised from the dead" (Goodspeed).†

1:5   "Through whom I have received the favour of my commission" (Moffatt).
       "Through him I received the privilege of a commission in his name" (NEB).‡

1:7   *Saints*—"dedicated people" (NEB).
       "Spiritual blessing and peace be yours from God" (Williams).§

ROMANS 1:8-17   PAUL AND HIS READERS

1:8   "I thank my God . . . because your faith *is being proclaimed* throughout the whole world." The verb is a compound and carries overtones of celebration and commendation. The present tense indicates an ongoing situation.
       But how should we understand the genitive case reflected in the English "your"? Is Paul exulting in the fact that the *object* of their faith, namely the gospel, is being proclaimed throughout the world, or is he paying tribute to the Christians in Rome by saying that their commitment to Christ (subjective case) is well known throughout the world? Might it even be that Paul is intentionally ambiguous in allowing us to consider both possibilities?
       Writing to Christians at Rome, Paul says their faith is known throughout "the whole world," but he likely expects his readers to understand that to be the "world" of the Roman Empire.

1:9   The verb translated "serve" is not the usual word for serve but one that carries overtones of spiritual service rendered to God (see Luke 2:37; Acts 7:42; Phil. 3:3; Heb. 9:9; 10:2).
       "In my spirit." In his human spirit.
       "Witness." (Gr. *martus*) Paul testifies to what he knows though it may mean his life.

---

*A *New Translation* (Moffat)
†*New Testament, An American Translation* (Goodspeed)
‡*New English Bible*
§Charles B. Williams, *The New Testament, A Translation in the Language of the People*

1:12   "That I may *encouraged together* with you . . . each of us by
        the other's faith." Since the verb translated "encouraged
        together" occurs only this time in the New Testament, it
        gives rise to various renderings. It is a compound verb, the
        root of which is the word so important in the gospel of John
        which also may be translated in a variety of ways, such as
        "comforter," "advocate," or "helper." Here the KJV trans-
        lates, "comforted together," the NIV,* "mutually encour-
        aged." "Be mutually helped" or "be strengthened together"
        would be equally appropriate.
        "By the other's faith" emphasizes that the apostle expects to
        be helped by the Christians at Rome as well as to be of help
        to them. The verb leaves the door open to understand this
        help to be in the form of comfort, admonition, or encour-
        agement. It could very well be that the verb is deliberately
        chosen with this rich variety of options in mind so that we
        should contemplate a grand mixture of blending them all.

1:13   *"I do not want you to be unaware."* This is Paul's way of
        saying, "I want you to know."

1:14   *"Greeks."* Those who spoke Greek and who had adopted
        Hellenistic culture.
        "Barbarians." All non-Greeks were considered barbarians.

1:16   *"Power."* (Gr. *dunamis*) The Greek word from which we get
        our word "dynamite."
        "Salvation." In the past: saved from the penalty of sin;
                       in the present: saved from the power of sin;
                       in the future: saved from the presence of sin.

1:17   *"Righteousness."* A God-kind of righteousness which in-
        cludes both justification and sanctification. The term
        "righteous" occurs ninety-one times in the twenty-seven
        books of the New Testament.
        "The righteous man shall live by faith." (cf., Hab. 2:4; Gal.
        3:11; Heb. 10:38).
        "The righteousness of God *is revealed.*" It is the *gospel*
        which reveals this righteousness of God, a righteousness
        which "is by faith from first to last" (NIV).

1:18   "The wrath of God *is revealed.*" The exact same form of the
        verb occurs in 1:17. The present tense is striking, for both
        are ongoing activities.

New International Version

Translations and Interpretations for Consideration

1:9　　"I call God to witness—to whom I render priestly and spiritual service by telling the Good News about His Son" (Weymouth).*

1:11　　"I want to bring you some spiritual gift to make you strong" (NEB).

1:14　　"To Greeks and to all other nations, to cultured and to uncultured people alike, I owe a duty" (Williams).

"I owe a debt both to Greeks and to foreigners, to the cultivated and the uncultivated" (Goodspeed).

1:17　　"For in the good news God's way of man's right standing with him is uncovered, the Way of faith that leads to greater faith" (Williams).

1:17　　"Because here is revealed God's way of righting wrong, a way that starts from faith and ends in faith" (NEB).

ROMANS 1:18-32　　THE PAGAN WORLD

1:18　　*"Wrath of God."* God's holy aversion to all that is evil.

1:20　　*"That which is known about God is evident within them; for God made it evident to them."* A paradox.

"His eternal power and *divine nature."* "Divine nature" translates just one word in the Greek text, a word that occurs only this time in the New Testament and means "Godhead" or "divinity." In Colossians 2:9 there is a similar word (differing only by the addition of one letter) which occurs only in that verse and means "Godhead" or "deity." The Colossian text makes it crystal-clear that God Himself (the divine *personality)* may be known only by revelation of Himself in His Son. Our text here, on the other hand, affirms that His divine *nature* and attributes may be known from His works.

1:24　　*"God gave them over."* Note the repetition of this in verses 26 and 28.

1:25a　　"They exchanged the truth of God for *a lie."* Literally, *the* lie. The "big lie." *The* big lie—that anything other than the almighty God may be worshiped—detracts from the glory that is His alone.

1:25b　　"Worshiped and served the creature *rather than* the Creator." "Alongside of" or "along with" would be a more

*Weymouth's New Testament in Modern Speech

literal translation. Satan's lie is more subtle than our English text suggests. The truth is that God cannot share that worship and service that belongs to Him alone.

1:25c   *"Amen."* This is the first of six times the apostle uses the "amen" to conclude a spontaneous and effervescent doxology. (Note the other occurrences in 9:5, 11:36, 15:33, 16:24, and 16:27.) This first doxology is particularly striking, surrounded as it is by such grim descriptions of the human heart.

1:28   *"And just as they did not see fit to acknowledge God any longer, God gave them over to a depraved mind."* From our English translations, one would never suspect that the italicized words are from the same root. This is a difficult verse to translate. Elsewhere in the New Testament, the verb clearly means "to test carefully" or "to examine critically." Surely it must convey something of thorough examination here as well. The adjective "depraved" is the negation of the activity suggested by the verb. It would ordinarily mean "untested" or, as a consequence, "rejected." Since man did not give himself to the appropriate careful search and investigation to discover God in His creation, God gave him over to the bent of his mind, which rejected God.

1:29   *"Strife"* translates a Greek word that means "party spirit," resulting in sharp argument and dissension. *"Malice"* is a word which occurs only here in the New Testament and suggests the tendency to put the worst construction on everything.
   "Being filled." This is a perfect participle indicating complete action with present results.

1:31   *"Without understanding, untrustworthy, unloving, unmerciful."* A good attempt to capture an obvious play on words as all four nouns in the Greek text begin with the same letter. Actually, there is a fifth such word as the last word in verse 30 ("disobedient") also begins with the same letter, thus initiating the series.

Translations and Interpretations for Consideration

1:18   "In their wickedness they are stifling the truth" (NEB).
1:19   "God is angry" (Weymouth).
1:20   "There is therefore no possible defence for their conduct" (NEB).

1:21   "But became absorbed in useless discussions, and their senseless minds were darkened" (Weymouth).
"They have turned to futile speculations till their ignorant minds grew dark" (Moffatt).
"They knew God and didn't honor Him as God or thank Him, but their thoughts turned to worthless things" (Beck).*

1:22   "While boasting of their wisdom they became utter fools" (Weymouth).

1:25   "Because they have bartered away the true God for a false one" (NEB).

1:30   "They are gossips, slanderers, abhorrent to God, insolent, overbearing, boastful, ingenious in evil, undutiful, conscienceless, treacherous, unloving, and unpitying" (Goodspeed).

1:31   "They are foolish. They break their promises. They have no love or mercy" (Beck).

ROMANS 2:1-16   THE MORALIST CONDEMNED

2:1   "You [Jews] are without excuse." We had the same word in 1:20 in relation to all men. Here the word is singular, and the singular *you* is emphatic. "For in that you judge another, you condemn yourself." As the first chapter began with a conscious effort in literary style, so does chapter 2. Again, it is a chiastic construction that does not come through in our English text. The word order actually is, "you judge the other fellow, yourself you condemn."

2:3   *"Do you suppose. . . ?"* The emphasis is upon the thinking process.

2:4   "The kindness of God leads you to *repentance.*" It is remarkable in view of the content of the entire epistle that this is the only time Paul uses the word "repentance," and that the verb "to repent" is not used at all. That is in spite of the fact that both are commonly used elsewhere in the New Testament.

2:5   "You are *storing up* wrath for yourself." The verb Paul uses suggests a deliberate use of irony, for the word really means "to accumulate treasure." The wickedness of man's heart is such that he treasures the very evil acts and thoughts that must bring down divine wrath upon him.

---

*New Testament in Language of Today

2:5-11 Whereas we have six sentences in our English text, there is just one tangled and rather difficult sentence in the Greek text. Which verb takes what object is not perfectly clear. It might be possible to translate verse 7, for example, "To those who seek eternal life, He will give glory and honor and immortality." The more one ponders this translation the more sense it makes, and it can be justified grammatically.

2:7 *"Doing good."* This is not stressing salvation by works, but is rather stressing the impartiality of God toward Jew and Gentile.

"Glory" and *"honor"* are concepts that are united both in Jewish and in Christian thought (see 1 Pet. 1:7; Rev. 4:9). "Glory" is always a difficult concept to define, though in this context it must be taken along with *honor* and *immortality* as describing the eternal life that God gives.

2:8 *"Wrath"* and *"indignation"* are essentially synonyms, both describing the attitude of God toward those on whom His judgment falls.

2:11 "For there is no *partiality* with God." Literally, "God does not accept anyone's face." It seems that this is one of few distinctively Christian words in that we have no record of its occurrence outside of the New Testament.

2:12 *"Without the law."* This is a reference to the Gentiles to whom the Mosaic law had not been given.

2:13 See Leviticus 18:5.

"The hearers of the law." Visualize the regular readings of the law in the synagogue and remember that there were few readers and many hearers. Compare this with what is said in verse 18 in the phrase "instructed by the law." The verb for instruction is the word from which we get our word "catechism" and indicates oral instruction.

2:14 *"They are a law for themselves"* does not imply that people can do whatever they want. The idea is that their actions testify that they know what is right and what is wrong.

2:15 *"Written in their hearts."* This is in contrast to the law written on tablets of stone.

Translations and Interpretations for Consideration

2:4 "Do you think so lightly of his wealth of kindness, forebearance, and patience, and fail to see that God's kindness ought to induce you to repent?" (Goodspeed).

"Do you not know his kindness is meant to make you repent?" (Moffatt).

"Or is it that you think slightingly of His infinite goodness, forebearance and patience, unaware that the goodness of God is gently drawing you to repentance?" (Weymouth).

2:9   "There will be grinding misery for every human being who is an evildoer" (NEB).

2:11   "For God has no favourites" (NEB).

2:13   "For merely hearing the Law read does not make a man upright in the sight of God; men must obey the Law to be made upright" (Goodspeed).

ROMANS 2:17-24   THE PERILS OF SELF-RIGHTEOUSNESS

2:17   *"Jew."* First found in 2 Kings 16:6. He was a son of Abraham (John 8:33).

2:17-18   *"If you bear the name Jew."* There are five claims to Jewish privileges. They rely upon the law, glory in God, knowing His will, approving things that are excellent, and being instructed in the law.

2:18   *"Approve the things that are essential."* The exact phrase is repeated in Philippians 1:10 where the NIV translates "discern what is best." This is one of the most intriguing phrases in the New Testament although it occurs only these two times. The verb is the one referred to in our note on 1:28 and means "to test and probe with exacting care." It may indeed mean "approve" as the NIV translates it, but to approve in the sense of putting our approval on that which has been carefully examined and rigorously tested. The noun in the phrase may mean "what is superior," but the root meaning is "that which differs." What is superior, we are to understand, is that which differs from the ordinary in an exemplary fashion. (The mark of Christian maturity according to Philippians 1:10 is that the Christian is able to "test things that differ" and so "approve what is superior.")

2:19   *"Confident."* To persuade (it is in the Greek perfect tense). This implies that a task was completed in the past in which a person came to a settled conviction.

2:20   *"Embodiment."* Rough sketch. This word occurs in only one other place in the New Testament (2 Tim. 3:5) and is translated "form."

The word translated "teacher" may also have the meaning

of "one who punishes," a meaning it does have in Hebrews 12:9, its only other occurrence in the New Testament. Some translators render this noun by a verb (Goodspeed, "train the foolish"). The term "foolish" refers more to moral than to intellectual weakness, and for this reason renderings such as "ignorant" (JB) and "stupid" (NEB) may be misleading to the reader. The concept of moral weakness may be expressed in some languages as "those whose hearts are weak" or "those whose hearts are twisted."[3]

2:22 *"Abhor."* This means to turn away from a thing because of the stench.

"Do you rob temples?" It seems that robbing pagan temples was a charge to which the Jews in their religious zeal were open. Josephus, the Jewish historian, warns his people against that practice.

2:23 It may be that we should understand this verse as a summary statement of the whole affair rather than as a question. Remember that punctuation marks were inserted into our texts in comparatively recent times. As a statement, it would read, "You who brag about the law, you dishonor God by breaking the law." Verse 24 would then stand as a quotation from the Old Testament supporting this summary.

2:24 *"Blasphemed."* Despised (See Isa. 52:5).

The Scripture to which Paul refers comes from Isaiah 52:5. As usual, Paul's quotation reflects the Septuagint translation rather than the Hebrew text.

Translations and Interpretations for Consideration

2:20 "A schoolmaster for the dull and ignorant" (Weymouth).
"An outline of real knowledge and an outline of the truth" (Weymouth).

ROMANS 2:25-29   OUTWARD AND INWARD

2:28 *"Outwardly."* Apparent, evident.
2:29 *"Inwardly."* Hidden, secret, concealed.

Translations and Interpretations for Consideration

2:29 "And real circumcision is heart-circumcision, a spiritual, not a literal affair" (Williams).
"A man is circumcised in his heart by the Spirit, not just by doing what the words say" (Beck).

ROMANS 3:1-8   IS THE WORLD LOST?

3:2-3   "They *were entrusted* with the oracles of God. What then? If
some *did not believe,* their *unbelief* will not nullify the *faithfulness* of God, will it?" Something is lost when our translations do not make apparent the fact that all the italicized
words derive from the same stem. Those four are key words
in this epistle. The first ("were entrusted") is the verb "to
believe" or "to trust" in the passive voice. This verb occurs
twenty-one times in Romans. The second ("did not believe")
is the same verb but with a negative prefix. This is the only
time it occurs in Romans. The third word ("unbelief") is the
negation of the common noun "belief" or "faith." This negative form occurs in three other places in our epistle. The
fourth word ("faithfulness") is the familiar word for "belief"
or "faith." It occurs a total of thirty-eight times in this epistle. It may be translated either "faith" or "faithfulness."
A very literal translation that makes obvious the relation of
the words each to the other may help: "They have been *entrusted* with the very words of God. What if some did not
keep the *trust?* Will their lack of *trust* nullify the *trustworthiness* of God?" Since the words are so rich and so central in
this letter, no translation really does justice. The crucial
thing to note is that far more than simple assent to fact is
involved in "belief." It is rather a matter of heart commitment.

3:2   We would expect Paul's expression *"first of all"* to introduce
a series of advantages that the Jews have. But, in fact he
mentions only one—their having been entrusted with the
very words of God. Later, in 9:4-5, Paul does mention other
advantages of the Jews.
"The oracles of God" are understood by some to be a reference to the entire Old Testament; others limit it to special
divine revelations as on Mount Sinai; others to the promises
of God in the Old Testament. However, the parallel passage
in 9:4 would seem to lend weight to taking it in the larger
sense of the entire Old Testament.

3:1-8   Note the interesting structure: objections, verses 1, 3, 5, 7, 8;
answers, verses 2, 4, 6.

3:3   *"The faithfulness of God."* The trustworthiness of God.

3:4   *"May it never be!"* A typically Pauline expression. Paul uses it thirteen times, and nine of those are in the epistle to the Romans. Only once is it used by a New Testament writer other than Paul (Luke 20:16). It is an exceedingly strong expression, and most appropriately the NIV uses an exclamation mark following it in every case except one. The variety of ways by which the NIV translates gives the reader a well-rounded idea of the meaning. Four times it is translated, "not at all!"; once "certainly not!"; three times, "by no means!"; once by the one word, "never!"; twice as, "absolutely not!"; and once it is translated by the phrase "may I never." The expression is found nine times in the book of Romans (3:4, 6, 31; 6:2, 15; 7:7; 9:14; 11:1, 6). It is found once in 1 Corinthians 6:15, and it occurs three times in Galatians (2:17, 21; 6:14).

"Let God be found true." Let God be *found* true is the idea. Obviously, God is always true.

"Every man be found a liar" is an allusion to Psalm 116:11, whereas the Scripture quotation in the last part of this verse is an exact quotation from Psalm 51:4 in the Septuagint. What we have is a court scene in which God always emerges victorious over his opponents because He is right.

3:5   This verse is in the form of a rhetorical question.

"Righteousness of God." The noun "unrighteousness" appears here also. (see also 1:18, 29; and 2:8.) Here "unrighteousness" stands in contrast to the "righteousness of God." Although the phrase "righteousness of God" is essentially the same phrase that Paul uses in 1:17, it is clear that Paul uses the phrase in a different sense in the present context. Whereas in the former passage it is used in the general Pauline sense of God's placing men in a right relationship with Himself, here it refers to an attribute of God, specifically the fact that God is right and does what is right. The various meanings of the term "righteousness" in this epistle to the Romans are dealt with later in this book in the section on devotional ideas. One must distinguish carefully between God's intrinsic righteousness, God's righteousness imputed, and the righteous walk to which the believer (to whom God's righteousness is imputed) is called.

3:7   *"The truth of God."* "God's truthfulness."

3:8   A literal rendering of the latter part of this verse might be "they are justly condemned."

Translations and Interpretations for Consideration

3:1   "What special privilege then, has a Jew? Or, what benefit
           does circumcision confer?" (Williams).
3:4   "Let God be true to His word, though every man be perfidi-
           ous" (Moffatt).
3:5   "Is God wrong (I'm talking like a man) when He's angry and
           He punishes?" (Beck).

ROMANS 3:9-20   THE WORLD CONDEMNED

3:9   *"Are we any better?"* Do we (the Jews) excel the Gentiles? is
           the idea. Interestingly, the verb may be either in the middle
           or passive voice, and either makes good sense. If we take it
           as middle, the force is: "Do we ourselves excel?" If we un-
           derstand it as passive, it would be translated: "Are we ex-
           celled?" In either case, the answer is a loud No! for both Jew
           and Gentile have been conclusively shown to be guilty.
           "Jews and Gentiles are all under sin." This affirmation is
           followed by fourteen negative points in verses 10-18.
3:10   The quotation is from Psalm 14:1-3. In the Psalm the first
           and sixth lines read the same, but Paul has made a signifi-
           cant change by introducing into the first line the word
           "righteous." By doing so Paul has departed from both the
           Hebrew and the Septuagint in order to introduce a term
           basic to his theology.
           For Paul this phrase would mean there is not a man who is
           in a right relationship with God. It is significant that in
           verse 20 Paul summarizes his total argument from the Scrip-
           tures by alluding to Psalm 143:2: *"By the works of the Law no
           flesh will be justified in His sight."*
3:10-12   Sin in human character (See Psalms 14:2-3; 53:2-3).
3:10-18   These verses contain indictment.
3:13   The first two lines of this verse come from Psalm 5:9. The
           last line of this verse is from Psalm 140:3.
3:13-17   Sin in human character (See Psalms 14:2-3; 53:2-3).
3:15   *"Shed."* To pour out.
3:18   This quotation is from Psalm 36:1.
3:19   The defense.
           "Know." We know absolutely.
           "Law." The Hebrew Scriptures in general. Paul has just
           summarized its content (vv. 10-18). He now reminds the Jews
           that the law applies, or more literally "speaks," to those

who live under the law, that is, to the Jews. Hence, the Jews themselves are guilty of the sins described in the preceding verses. It has already been shown that the Gentiles stand condemned under God's judgment, and now the Jews also are shown to be equally guilty in God's sight. The purpose of the law is clearly to nullify all human excuses and bring the whole world under God's judgment.

3:19-20 The verdict. Verse 20 is a free quotation and amplification of Psalm 143:2. (See Acts 13:39 and 1 Tim. 1:9-10.)

3:20 In quoting Psalm 143:2, Paul adds *by the works of the Law.* This phrase refers to those things done in obedience to the law and that may be looked upon as a means of securing a right relationship with God.

"Justified" is the same verb that was used in 1:16 and will be discussed again in 3:24. Again, Paul reminds everyone that the purpose of the law is not to give salvation but to make men conscious that they have sinned.

Translations and Interpretations for Consideration

3:9 "For we have already charged all Jews and Gentiles alike with being in thraldom to sin" (Weymouth).

3:17 "They are strangers to the high-road of peace" (NEB).

3:20 "Law simply brings a sure knowledge of sin" (Weymouth).

ROMANS 3:21-31   REDEMPTION IN CHRIST

3:21-26 These verses constitute one sentence of unusual theological significance. The NIV divides them into five sentences and inserts a dash between verses 25 and 26, indicating broken or awkward syntax. A drastic change in punctuation makes the sentence flow more freely and preserves the argument. With a parenthesis before "there is no difference" in verse 22, and the closing parenthesis at the end of verse 23, verses 22-25 will now read as one sentence. So one of the best known verses of Scripture (verse 23) is really parenthetical. One of the things that makes this sentence difficult is that the phrase "righteousness of God" occurs four times, and it does not always mean the same thing. In verse 22 it is the righteousness of God imputed to the believer, whereas in verse 25 it is the *intrinsic* righteousness of God. The NIV makes that distinction apparent, but only at the expense of substituting another word ("justice") for "righteousness" of the Greek text.

Another example of how careful the reader must be is that the word "Law" occurs twice in verse 21 with two very different meanings. In the first instance it is clearly the law *principle* Paul has in mind, whereas in the second instance "the Law" associated as it is with the "The Prophets" clearly refers to the *books* of the law. So the righteousness that is apart from the law is indeed witnessed to by the law. This leaves no contradiction since *"testify"* is a present tense participle indicating that this witness is a continuing experience.

3:21   *"But now."* A logical, not temporal transition.

"Has been manifested." A revelation not discovered by man, but rather an unveiling of God.

3:23   *"For all have sinned and fall short."* The two verbs are in different tenses and that is important. The tense of the first indicates a clear, established fact—all have sinned. The second, however, is in the present tense and suggests an ongoing condition. Not only have all sinned, but all are continually falling short of the glory of God.

3:24   *"Being justified as a gift by His grace."* (This word occurs in only one other place in the New Testament, John 15:25, where it is said of Jesus that He was hated "without a cause.") There is no reason or intrinsic worth in man that he should be justified.

"Justified." The legal act of God declaring the guilty guiltless. It represents a change of standing before God. This is the language of the law court. "Justify" is one of the most significant verbs in the book of Romans. The verb has already been seen three times (2:13; 3:4, 20). The related noun has been seen four times (1:17; 3:5, 21-22). The verb is a legal or judicial term meaning "to make right" or "to declare right." Paul's analogy is that of the law court. It is not that God's pronouncement makes men morally right, but that God pronounces men acquitted or not guilty in His sight to put man into a right relationship with Himself.

"Redemption." Release by ransom. New Testament illustrations include: to buy in the slave market (1 Cor. 6:20); to buy out of the slave market (Gal. 3:13); to set free by paying a price (Titus 2:14).

"Through the redemption which is in Christ Jesus." Although "redemption" is a noun in the Greek, this word is translated in a variety of ways in the different translations—for exam-

ple, "ransom" (Moffatt), "by being redeemed" (JB), "deliverance" (Goodspeed), and "act of liberation" (NEB).

3:25 *"Propitiation."* This is that which provides satisfaction for a broken law. We are justified by: grace (3:24); blood (v. 25); and faith (v. 28).

"In the forbearance of God He passed over the sins previously committed." (For treatment of this troublesome concept, see "Does God Overlook Sin?" in the section on devotional ideas in this volume.)

3:27 *"By what kind of law?"* The NIV translates "On what principle?" (Same word as above, see note on 3:21-26). When Paul here uses the phrase, "the law of faith," one naturally suspects he is doing so ironically, as the thrust of his argument has been to distinguish clearly between law and faith.

Translations and Interpretations for Consideration

3:22 "God's own way of giving men right standing with Himself is through faith in Jesus Christ" (Williams).

3:24 "But by his mercy they are made upright for nothing, by the deliverance secured through Christ Jesus" (Goodspeed).

3:25 "He it is whom God put forward as a Mercy-Seat, rendered efficacious through faith in His blood" (Weymouth).

3:31 "Does this mean that we are using faith to undermine law? By no means: we are placing law itself on a firmer footing" (NEB).

ROMANS 4:1-8   JUSTIFICATION BY FAITH

4:3 *"It was reckoned* to him as righteousness." This is, without doubt, the key word in chapter 4. The verb reflected in our translation as "was reckoned" occurs a total of thirty-nine times in the New Testament. Of these, nineteen times are in the epistle to the Romans and eleven are in Romans 4. The term is almost a mathematical one and can mean "count" or "calculate." The powerful truth of chapter 4 is that by simple faith in Christ His righteousness is imputed to us, credited to our account, and noted down on our side of the ledger (See Gen. 15:6).

4:4-5 These verses illustrate and explain the Scripture quotation given in verse 3. Verse 4 is an illustration from everyday life: the man who works receives his wages from something he has earned, not as a gift.

4:5   The contrast between *works and wages* and *faith and grace* is made clear. It is the faith of the believer that God takes into account, not the works of the man who tries to earn his own salvation.

4:6-8   The outcome of faith (See Psalm 32).

4:7   *"Covered."* As with a shroud (only here in the New Testament).

ROMANS 4:9-16   JUSTIFIED BY GRACE

4:9   The question which Paul raises in this verse marks an important transition in his argument. According to certain Jewish rabbis, the blessings described in Psalm 32 and quoted by Paul above applied only to the Jewish people. Paul now proceeds to demonstrate that the blessedness referred to in the Psalm applies not only to the Jewish people, but also to the Gentiles as well.

4:9-12   Note the interesting development of personal righteousness: question (v. 9); answer (v. 10); proof (v. 11); and purpose (vv. 11-12).

4:12   *"Who . . . follow in the steps."* Both the verb "follow" and the noun "steps" are unusual words. In a military context, the verb would imply "walking in file."
The JB translates this *"follow . . . along the path of faith,"* while the NEB has *"walk in the footprints of the faith."* The expression "to walk" is frequently used in the Old Testament and in the New to mean "live one's life."

4:13-16   Note the illustration of representative righteousness: the promise (v. 13); the principle (v. 15); the proof (v. 16).

4:14   "For if those who are of the law are heirs, faith *is made void* and the promise *is nullified."* Both of the verbs are in the perfect tense, so literally, "faith *has been made empty* [or vain] and the promise *has been made invalid."*

4:15   "For the Law *brings* about wrath." The verb is an intensive compound. "Works down" is the literal rendering. The compound gives the verb an intensive emphasis something like "grinds out wrath."
Note that the word "law" occurs twice in this short verse and that it seems to designate two different things. Paul's first reference to *law* in this verse has the definite article, "the law." This is most naturally taken to mean the (Jewish) law. The second reference to *law* is a reference to law in general, and not to the Jewish law in particular.

Translations and Interpretations for Consideration

4:9　　"Now does this happiness come to the Jews alone, or to the heathen people too?" (Williams).

4:14　　"If the Law is the way to get it, then faith can't get anything and the promise can't give anything" (Beck).

ROMANS 4:17-25　　AN ILLUSTRATION OF FAITH

4:17　　Faith must be centered in a person (See Gen. 17:5).
　　　　"Calls into being that which does not exist." This ties in well with the preceding phrase. While the Greek text is ambiguous, faith is not fiction.

4:25　　*"Because of our justification."* Christ's resurrection was a proof of God's acceptance of His Son's sacrifice.

Translations and Interpretations for Consideration

4:18　　"Abraham, building on hope in spite of hopeless circumstances" (Williams).

4:20　　"His faith won strength as he gave glory to God and felt convinced that He was able to do what He had promised" (Moffatt).
　　　　"There was no unbelief to make him doubt what God promised, but by faith he got strong and gave glory to God" (Beck).

4:21　　"He was fully convinced God could do what He promised" (Beck).

4:24　　"Faith, before long, will be placed to the credit of us also who are believers in Him who raised Jesus, our Lord, from the dead" (Weymouth).

ROMANS 5:1-11　　THE SECURITY OF THE JUSTIFIED

　　　　Romans 5 begins a new section in the letter. That can be seen not only by the solemn conclusion of 4:23-25, but also by the content of chapter 5 itself.

5:1-11　*Hope—The security of the justified*
　　　　5:1-2　　Present experience assures it.
　　　　5:3-5　　Affliction cannot destroy it.
　　　　5:6-10　God's love through the gift of His Son confirms it.
　　　　5:11　　God crowns our hope.

5:1   *"Peace with God."* To bind together what has been separated.

"Therefore, since we have been justified through faith, *we have* peace with God." There has been a great deal of disagreement about this verb. The manuscripts disagree among themselves. Some have the indicative mood as do our translations, while others have the subjunctive mood. If we take the verb to be subjunctive, we would then translate not "we have," but rather "let us have." In the one case it is the *result* of our being justified and in the other it is an *admonition* based on the fact of our justification. In either case, the verb is in the present tense indicating that peace should be our continuing possession.

Both in the Old Testament and in the New Testament the term *peace* has a broad range of meaning. It describes the harmonious relationship between man and God on the basis of God's having put man right with Himself.

5:2   *"Exult in hope of the glory of God."* A better translation would be: "We boast in the hope of the glory which God will manifest."

"Exult." Note the repetition of this word in verses 3 and 11. The verb translated *"exult"* has as its basic meaning "to boast." The first person plural indicative and the subjunctive of this verb are identical in form, so that the meaning may be either "we exult," a statement of fact, or "let us exult," an exhortation. The indicative is more in keeping with the context. Paul is not exhorting his readers to behave as they should as Christians. Instead, he is reminding them of what is already theirs to enjoy in Christ.

The meaning of the word *"glory"* is more difficult. Originally the word meant "heavy" or "weighty" and later came to be used in the specific sense of the revelation of some heavenly being, especially of God himself. So when Paul speaks of "the glory of God" he has in mind the revelation of what God is like, that is, God's own character.[4]

"Through whom also *we have obtained* our introduction by faith into this grace in which *we stand;* and *we exult* in the hope of the glory of God." The sequence of the tenses of the verbs is significant. The first two verbs are in the perfect tense signifying something completed in past time with results carrying over into the present. "We *have obtained*" access (and now enjoy it); we have been (and now are) established. But now the third verb is in the present tense, giving us the ongoing result of the two previous verbs. We do continually exult in the hope of the glory of God.

Paul's word *"stand"* appears as "live" in the TEV. It is more appropriate in English to speak of living an experience than of standing in one.

5:3 *"Tribulations."* Pressure or affliction.

5:4 The word rendered *"character"* is a relatively rare term and is used only by Paul in the New Testament, seven times in all. This word is related to the verb used in 2:18, and it describes something that is put to the test and then is approved if it passes the test. Something of both testing and approval are involved, and it is God who makes the judgment. This word implies close scrutiny and rigorous examination as well as the character of excellence of that which passes the best.

5:5 *"And hope does not disappoint."* The verb Paul used here seems almost too strong, but "disappoint" or "does not prove illusory" surely miss the force of the verb. The verb really means "to disgrace," "to dishonor," or "put to shame."

5:6, *"While we were still helpless, ... while we were yet sinners,*
8, 10 *... while we were enemies."* Since all three expressions represent the same grammatical construction, it would seem that Paul is asking us to note a crescendo of depravity in his description of man's spiritual state.

5:6 In the phrase *"for the ungodly,"* the preposition "for" must be taken with the meaning of "for the sake of," and not with the meaning "in place of." In the present passage Paul is dealing with the extent to which God went in order to show His love for sinful man.

5:7 *"Good."* Noble.
"Would dare even to die" must be understood more in a sense of "might be willing to die."

5:9 *"Much more."* Note the repetition of this phrase in verses 10, 15, 17, and 20.
"By His blood." Here, as elsewhere in the New Testament, "blood" is used of Christ's violent death, and so has the same meaning that it does in 3:25. When Paul speaks of "the blood of Christ," he is, of course, drawing from the language of the Old Testament sacrificial system.

5:10 This verse contains two parallel clauses, and so is similar in form to the structure of 4:25. It is a conditional sentence which is understood to be true to fact, and so may be translated as a statement: "We were enemies."

As in verse 9, the expression *"much more"* may be rendered "obviously," or, "it must surely be the case."

Translations and Interpretations for Consideration

5:1   "Since we have been given right standing with God through faith, then let us continue enjoying peace with God through our Lord Jesus Christ" (Williams).

5:2   "And we feel proud as we hope for God's glory" (Beck).

5:3   "More than that, we ought to glory in our troubles" (Goodspeed).

5:4   "And endurance, tested character, and tested character, hope" (Williams).

        "Suffering produces fortitude; fortitude, ripeness of character" (Weymouth).

5:5   "Such a hope is no mockery, because God's love has flooded our inmost heart through the Holy Spirit he has given us" (NEB).

5:7   "Though once in a while a man is brave enough to die for a generous friend" (Williams).

5:11   "Who has now given us this friendship" (Beck).

ROMANS 5:12-21   THE FOUNDATION OF RIGHTEOUSNESS

5:12-21 Note the six sets of contrasts:

         Adam and Christ (vv. 14-15)

         Condemnation and justification (v. 16)

         Disobedience and obedience (v. 19)

         Law and grace (v. 20)

         Sin and righteousness (v. 21)

         Death and life (v. 21).

"Sin" and *"death"* are words which occur frequently in this paragraph and throughout chapter 6 as well. Usually the definite article is used with them. Perhaps there is the suggestion that they should be personified. If we capitalize them, we catch something of the flavor intended. In verse 12, they are pictured as two monsters entering the world — first sin, and then death.

5:12   *"World."* The cosmos. It is the same word as appears in John 3:16.

5:12a   *"One man."* There is a typical Pauline break in the pattern of thought. Note that he does not take up the "one man" again until verse 15.

5:12b   "Death *spread* to all men." The compound form of the verb suggests that death came to "pervade" all men.

5:13   "Sin is not imputed." The verb is a bookkeeping term. In the New Testament it is used only here and in Philemon 18, where the NASB translates it "charge that to my account."

5:14-21 Death reigned (v. 14).
Believers shall reign (v. 17).
Sin reigned (v. 21).
Grace reigns (v. 21).

5:14   "*Adam*." He was a type of Christ (1 Cor. 15:27, 45).
"A *type* of Him who was to come." The literal meaning of the word is "the imprint or mark left when a blow has been struck." The theological use of the word would be to indicate an event or a person in history corresponding in certain respects to another event or person.
"Who had not sinned *in the likeness of the offense of Adam*." Here the NASB and the KJV translate literally. The NIV interprets for us that Adam's offense was disobedience.

5:15-21 Note the contrasts and comparisons in this closely reasoned paragraph. The most obvious contrast is the "one" against the "many." This contrast is explicitly drawn in verses 15-19. Within the "one" there is a contrast between Adam and Christ and the decisive act of each. Then there is the contrast between sin and grace. Sin is the result of Adam's act of transgression; grace is the result of Christ's act of obedience.

Sin and grace are not simply contrasted, but each member of the contrast is elaborated. There are in the paragraph four words for sin and four words for grace. (Actually, one of the words for sin is found in the last phrase of v. 14). The first word for sin (v. 14) speaks of sin as an act of transgression, a deliberate going beyond the boundary set by God. The second word (twice in v. 15, once each in vv. 16, 17, 18, 19, 20) means a lapse or deviation from God's standard, a falling alongside of God's command. The third word (once each in vv. 20 and 21, the cognate participle in v. 16, and the personal form of the noun in v. 19) is the most common word for sin in the New Testament. It means failure to attain God's design and goal for man; a falling short of what is pleasing to God. The fourth word (v. 19) indicates man's failure to hear what God says, which leads him to disobey.

There are also four words for grace in this paragraph. The familiar word "grace" appears twice; a related noun meaning "something given by grace" occurs twice (vv. 15-16); two nouns from the verb "to give" also occur (one in v. 15 and the other in v. 16). In the NIV, the word "gift" occurs three times in verses 15 and 16. The RSV* has "free gift" in each place. The NASB has "free gift" for the first and "gift" for the last two. Actually, the Greek text has three different words, although the last two are from the same root. Since the first is from the same stem as "grace" and the last two from the stem "to give," the NASB catches the distinction fairly well.

5:13-15   Within the space of three verses, Paul uses three different words for "sin." The first suggests sin in its nature, whereas the second and third refer to sin as specific acts of transgression.

5:15   *"Transgression."* A deviation from the right path.

5:19   *"Disobedience."* This is one of nine words for sin in the New Testament. It is made up of words meaning "to hear alongside." Trench says that it means "a failing to hear."

5:20   *"Law."* There is no article before "law." The law does not frustrate, but it furthers the work of Christ.

5:20a   *"The law came in."* Literally, the law "came in alongside." With the standard of God's law placed alongside our sin, we see how odious our sin actually is.

5:20b   *"Grace abounded all the more."* The verb is a compound form and is much like the English "super." Grace "super-abounded."

5:21   *"Reigned."* Sin is personified.

Translations and Interpretations for Consideration

5:15   "But God's act of grace is out of all proportion to Adam's wrongdoing" (NEB).

5:20   "But greatly as sin multiplied, God's mercy has far surpassed it" (Goodspeed).

ROMANS 6:1-14   OUR UNION WITH CHRIST

6:1   *"To continue."* To remain or abide.

"Shall we *continue* in sin. . . ?" The compound form of the

---

*Revised Standard Version

verb suggests that a deliberate commitment to sin is what is contemplated.

6:2 *"How."* How is it possible? (Rhetorical).

"How shall we who died to sin live in it?" The sequence of the tenses suggests that the dying was a decisive crisis experience, and the living an ongoing state.

6:3 *"Baptized."* This is a transliteration of the Greek word.

6:4 *"Live a new life."* To order one's behavior.

6:5 *"If."* A fulfilled condition: "in view of the fact."

6:6 *"Old."* Worn out.

"Crucified." An aorist tense signifying past action.

"Done away with." Not annihilated, but reduced to impotence (2 Thess. 2:8).

"That our body of sin might *be done away with.*" The verb is a difficult one to translate as evidenced by the fact that of the twenty-seven occurrences in the New Testament, it is translated no less than eighteen different ways in the KJV and by sixteen different words or phrases in the NIV. Not simply the same verb, but the identical form of the verb is translated in three quite different ways within the space of three verses in our NIV rendering of 1 Corinthians 13:8-10: "prophecies . . . *will cease"* (v. 8); "knowledge . . . *will pass away"* (v. 8); and "the imperfect *disappears"* (v. 10). Clearly, "to cease," "to pass away" and "to disappear" are far from conveying one and the same connotation. One of the uses of the verb with which we are dealing was as a medical term which meant "to make numb" or "to paralyze." "Render powerless" of the NIV here catches something of that flavor.

6:11-13 The commands are intriguing. Note that two are positive and two are negative (prohibitions). First is a positive command (v. 11), "count" or "reckon." But it is in the imperative mood, so "do it" is the idea. Then there are two prohibitions, "do not let sin reign" (v. 12) and "do not . . . present" (v. 13). Last is another positive command (v. 13), "do offer."

The tenses are most significant and our translations do not bring this out. The first three are in the present tense: "continue to consider yourselves dead to sin," "do not let sin continue to reign," and "do not go on presenting the parts of your body to sin." But the tense of the final command shifts to suggest that, by a definitive act, we are to offer ourselves to God.

6:11 *"Consider."* Calculate by adding up the facts in verses 1-10.

6:12   *"Reign."* Exercise kingly power.

6:13   We are to offer the total parts of our bodies as members to God, not to sin. The word translated "members" is, more literally, "weapons," The KJV renders the verb, "present." As our Lord reviews His troops, we are to *present arms,* the "arms" being our very bodies.

"To be used for wicked purposes" and *"to be used for righteous purposes"* can be rendered very literally as "instruments of wickedness" and "instruments of righteousness."[5]

Translations and Intrepretations for Consideration

6:13   "Don't let sin keep on using your organs as tools for doing wrong" (Beck).

6:14   "For now you are not living as slaves to law but as subjects to God's favor" (Williams).

ROMANS 6:15—7:6   OUR IDENTIFICATION WITH CHRIST

6:1-23   Note a unique structure: a rhetorical question (v. 1); an answer (vv. 2-14); a rhetorical question (v. 15); and an answer (vv. 16-23).

6:16   *"Slaves."* Servants. This is the most servile term for a slave in the Greek language ("doulos"). This word means one whose will is swallowed up in the will of another. It also refers to one who is bound to another so strongly that only death can free. A third meaning is one who serves another to the disregard of his own interests.

"Death" in the New Testament carries a variety of meanings depending upon the context. Paul uses the word to mean the "spiritual death" of all men in their natural state apart from Christ (see Eph. 2:1; Col. 2:13), and "eternal death" as the final judgment of God on the life of sin (Rom. 6:16).

6:17   *"From the heart"* appears in other translations as "wholehearted" (NEB), "without reservation" (JB), and "sincerely" (NAB).*

6:19   *"Impurity"* and *"lawlessness"* were two sins that the Jews thought of as distinctive of the Gentile world.

6:22   *"You derive your benefit."* There is an ambiguity in the Greek text which could be deliberate. The verb may be either in the indicative mood as our NIV translates it, or it

---

*The New American Bible

may be in the imperative mood and then would be: "But now that you have been set free from sin and become slaves to God, *reap* your benefit unto holiness." Or, since the verb is in the present tense: "continue to reap (or enjoy) your benefit (or fruit) unto holiness."

6:23   *"Wages."* The part of a soldier's support given to him as pay.

7:1-6   Paul introduces a new metaphor. The Christian, because of his death with Christ, is free from his marriage to the law and is brought into a new marriage with Christ.

7:1   *"Know the law."* The legal principles, not the Mosaic law.

7:5   *"While we were in the flesh."* When we were unregenerated.

"For while we were in the flesh." The word "flesh" behind our translations at this point may carry a variety of connotations. We see this quite dramatically within the book of Romans. In 1:3 and 9:3-8, the word clearly means *blood relationship.* The NIV translates "human nature" in 1:3. In 2:28 it clearly refers to the *physical body.* The NIV translates "physical." In 3:20 it is used to designate *humanity.* The NIV renders it "no one." Here in 7:5 it has yet a different connotation. The NIV translates it "sinful nature"; the NASB and the KJV translate it according to the basic meaning of the word as "flesh," thereby leaving the reader to determine its more precise connotation. Clearly here it does mean our old nature.

"For when we were controlled by our sinful nature" is literally "for when we were in the flesh." Note how the translations differ: "when we were unspiritual" (Moffatt); "while we lived on the level of our lower nature" (NEB); "for when we were living mere physical lives" (Goodspeed). In the present passage "life in the flesh" is life lived apart from the control of God's Spirit (see v. 6); it describes life lived according to one's own human nature and which is under the law, sin, and death.

7:6   *"Oldness."* That which is worn out.

Translations and Interpretations for Consideration

6:21   "What was your advantage then in doing the things that make you blush now?" (Beck).

6:22   "But now that you have been set free from the tyranny of Sin" (Weymouth).

7:7-13   Note the revelations of the law:
   The law reveals the fact of sin (v. 7).
   The law reveals the occasion of sin (v. 8).
   The law reveals the power of sin (v. 9).
   The law reveals the deceitfulness of sin (v. 11).
   The law reveals the sinfulness of sin (vv. 12-13).

7:7-25   Note the personal pronoun "I." Eight times within this section the personal pronoun is heavily emphasized by Paul as he, rather than simply incorporating it into the verb, dramatically repeats it. While this device is not discernible in our translations, it indicates the dramatic way Paul is here reliving a crucial period in his life.

7:7   *"Know"* is used, not in the sense of theoretical knowledge, but to indicate a concrete experience. It will be helpful to expand this statement further. All men are selfish and inwardly rebellious against God. However, sin cannot be brought to light in such a way that it can be seen and measured apart from its rejection of a specific commandment of God. This is what Paul means by "knowing sin"; he rejected God's command and so became conscious of himself as a sinful being. He uses the specific example of the tenth commandment to illustrate what he means. He would never *have known what it is to covet if the Law had not said, "Do not covet."* [6]

The word translated "covet" means literally "desire" and is sometimes used in the New Testament in a good sense (see Luke 22:15), but generally it is found with evil connotations. Paul is here following a rather typical Jewish viewpoint, which speaks of the three stages of desire, sin, and death (cf., James 1:15). [7]

7:8-20   The verb translated by the NASB as "produce" or "do" occurs six times within these verses. It is a compound verb with heavy or destructive overtones. Compare the way it is used in Romans 1:27; 2:9; 4:15. Also, its use by Paul in 1 Corinthians 5:3 is instructive.

7:8   In the phrase *"sin, taking the opportunity,"* the word "opportunity," translates a term which originally was used by the military to mean "a base of operation." In its seven occurrences in the New Testament it is used in a metaphorical sense with the meaning of "opportunity (to do something)." Here law was not intended to be the means by which sin would launch its attack, but sin took advantage of this opportunity to attack man.

7:11   *"Taking the opportunity"* translates the same phrase found in verse 8, and the exegesis of this verse is similar to that of verse 8. For Paul, it is sin that deceived him.

"Sin . . . *deceived* me." The verb could be rendered very literally, "to throw one off the track."

7:12   Without question the word *"Law"* in this verse refers to the Jewish law. The *"Law is holy"* for it is God's law. The *"commandment is holy"* and *"righteous"* for it is God's commandment and it tells me what God says is right and *"good,"* for God intends it for my good.

7:13   "That through the commandment sin might become *utterly* sinful." The word behind the English word "utterly" is the word from which we get our English "hyperbole."

The final sentence in verse 13 indicates purpose. In this context, however, it can also be treated as result; for example, "so that through the commandment sin might become utterly sinful" (NIV), or "because the commandment says one should not sin, sin becomes even worse." Sin, using God's good law, brought death. As a result, sin's true nature is revealed.

7:14-25 Note the unique structure:

    The first confession (vv. 14-17)

        Statement (v. 14)

        Proof (vv. 15-16)

        Conclusion (v. 17)

    The second confession (vv. 18-20)

        Statement (v. 18)

        Proof (vv. 18-19)

        Conclusion (v. 20)

    The third confession (vv. 21-25)

        Statement (v. 21)

        Proof (vv. 22-23)

        Conclusion (vv. 24-25).

There are forty-seven personal pronouns within nineteen verses.

7:14   *"Sold."* Perfect tense. Foreclosed the mortgage and owns the slave.

7:15-25 This is the diagnosis of what happens when one tries to be sanctified by keeping the law.

7:16   *"Good."* Morally good.
7:17   *"Sin which indwells me."* The word order in the original
        lends a striking force to the phrase as the definite article
        "the" is separated from the noun "sin" by the phrase "in-
        dwells me." A literal translation would be "the living-in-me
        sin." A graphic description of man's total depravity.
7:18   For some languages *"in my flesh"* is equivalent to "in my
        heart." But in most instances, more appropriate expressions
        are "in me as just a human being," "in me as just a man," or
        "in the man that I am."
7:24   *"Wretched."* Exhausted through hard labor.

Translations and Interpretations for Consideration

7:18   "I can will, but I cannot do, what is right" (Goodspeed).

ROMANS 8:1-4   DELIVERANCE BY THE POWER OF THE HOLY SPIRIT

8:1   The glorious fact.
        *"There is therefore now no condemnation for those who are
        in Christ Jesus."* The KJV adds, "who walk not after the
        flesh, but after the Spirit." Some late manuscripts read that
        way. It is as if the thought that justification simply on the
        merits of Christ is too good to be true, so human effort and
        qualification are introduced. But, *no!* The "no" here
        suggests that there is not even one little bit of condemna-
        tion for the one who is in Christ.
8:2   The perfect explanation.
        "Spirit of life" is taken by most commentators to mean "the
        Spirit, which brings us life" (see NEB, "the life-giving law of
        the Spirit"), or "the Spirit which causes us truly to live."
        Paul continues to play on the word "law" in the phrases *"the
        law of the Spirit of life"* . . . *"and the law of sin and of death."*
        Clearly, "law" here means "principle."
8:3   The divine cause.
        "He condemned sin *in the flesh."* All must agree that this is
        precisely what the Greek text states. But what does "in the
        flesh" mean? Here we take it to mean "in his own flesh."
        1 Peter 2:24 reads, "He Himself bore our sins *in His body* on
        the cross."
8:4   The practical purpose.
        Verses 3 and 4 are just one sentence in the Greek text, and

verse 4 begins with a conjunction which may be understood to indicate either purpose or result.

"*Requirements of the Law*" translates a singular form in the Greek text. It is a collective noun so the idea is "the righteous deeds which the law demands."

Translations and Interpretations for Consideration

8:4 "For our lives are regulated not by our earthly, but by our spiritual natures" (Weymouth).
"Since we live not on the physical, but on the spiritual plane" (Goodspeed).

ROMANS 8:5-17 THE POWER OF SANCTIFICATION

8:5-6 Note the two principles and the two tendencies.

8:5 "For those who are according to the flesh *set their minds* on the things of the flesh." It is difficult to translate this verb since it conveys something of both thinking and willing. It is a matter of focusing one's thoughts in a certain direction and then striving for it. See note on Romans 12:3.
"Flesh" may well denote the body so that we could translate "those who live as the body dictates, find their minds controlled by their bodily desires." More likely, we should understand "flesh" to mean "fleshly desires."

8:9-17 Note the sufficiency of the Spirit for the believers: the believer's power (vv. 9-11); the believer's purity (vv. 12-15); and the believer's prospect (vv. 16-17).

8:9 "*If* the Spirit of God dwells in you." "If" is better translated "since."

8:10a "The body is *dead* because of sin." Subject to death or smitten with death.
"The body is *dead* because of sin, yet the spirit is alive." "Dead" is an adjective, but "alive" is a noun. Through the Holy Spirit the very life of God is in man not merely as an attribute (adjective), but inherent in his nature (noun). Also, in the next verse, "spirit" is identified as the Spirit of God.

8:13 "*Putting to death the deeds of the body.*" Paul is affirming that life lived under the direction of God's Spirit will be evident in the believer's daily life.
The metaphor is very powerful. Literally, the text reads "kill the deeds of the body." "Put an end to your sinful actions" is the idea.

8:15   *"Adoption."* The act of God which places the believer in His family as an adult son. His position is one of privilege; his practice involves growth in grace.
"Abba." Aramaic for "father."
"Cry." As with a loud voice.
There are two different words for *Father* in this verse. One is Aramaic and the other is Greek. Most translators transliterate the "Abba" and translate the "Father." "Abba" has overtones of endearment and affection. "Daddy" might not be a bad translation.

8:16-17   Note the witness and the blessing of the Spirit.

8:17   *"Suffer with Him"* is one word in the Greek text and it is used only one other time in the New Testament (in 1 Cor. 12:26).
"Glorified with Him" is also one word and occurs nowhere else in the New Testament.
There is a nice play on words here as "co-heirs" begins with the same sound as the two verbs above.

Translations and Interpretations for Consideration

8:9   "But that is not how you live. You are on the spiritual level, if only God's Spirit dwells within you; and if a man does not possess the Spirit of Christ, he is no Christian" (NEB).

8:17   "If we share his sufferings now in order to share his splendour hereafter" (NEB).

ROMANS 8:18-25   THE PRODUCTS OF SANCTIFICATION

8:18   *"Consider."* Calculate.
In *"to be revealed,"* the understood agent is God; that is, God is going to reveal it to us and in us. By "revealed" we should understand that which Christians will experience, not merely something they will see with their eyes.

8:19   *"Waits eagerly."* Earnest expectation (only here and in Phil. 1:20).
"The anxious longing of the creation *waits eagerly."* All of this is the translation of just one word in the Greek text. The etymology may suggest something like "watching with outstretched head" and, therefore, to watch anxiously.

8:20   *"In hope."* Upon the basis of hope.
"For the creation was subjected *to futility."* It is the idea of looking for what one does not find and hence futility, frustration, and disappointment.

The word translated "futility" stands first in the Greek text to emphasize its important use. In the New Testament this word appears elsewhere only in Ephesians 4:17.

8:21　*"Into the freedom of the glory."* In such a context one would normally understand the genitive "of glory" to be equivalent to an adjective "glorious."

8:23　*"First fruits."* First installment.

"We . . . having *the first fruits of the Spirit."* Here we are to understand not that the believer now has some first fruit of the Spirit and others will come later, but rather that the Holy Spirit is the firstfruit of our future glory. That is, the Holy Spirit Himself is the firstfruit or promise of what is to follow.

8:24　*"Hope."* Notice the emphasis by repetition. The noun occurs three times and the verb once in this brief verse. Since "hope" in the New Testament means "confident expectation," and since in the phrase "in this hope we have been saved," the definite article is used. "Hope" here is close in meaning to "faith."

Translations and Interpretations for Consideration

8:19　"Nature is waiting on tiptoe to see the unveiling of God's family" (Beck).

8:23　"More than that. Since the Spirit whom we have is our first taste of heaven" (Beck).

ROMANS 8:26-34　　THE PRIVILEGE OF PRAYER

8:26　*"Helps."* By carrying part of the load.

"The Spirit also *helps* our weakness." This is a most interesting double compound verb. (It is used in the New Testament only here and in Luke 10:40 where Martha complains to the Lord and suggests He ask her sister to *help* her.) The prepositions in the compound are important. The first suggests "along with" and the other "over against." The Holy Spirit lays hold of our weakness *along with us* and carries his part of the burden *over against* us as if two men were carrying a piece of furniture with one at each end.

8:28　*"Love."* Are loving.

"And we know that God causes *all things* to work together for good." Compare with the KJV, "all things work together for good." Here, the NASB is to be preferred. The word "God" is in the oldest manuscripts and grammatically it must stand as the subject. Note that the KJV makes "all things" the subject. There is no word for "in" in the Greek text. Rather, "all things" must stand as the object of the verb. So there is no magic involved, but rather the sovereignty of God is controlling and working out "all things."

8:29-30 In these two verses Paul uses a series of five verbs to describe the divine purpose. Each verb builds on the preceding one and leads to the following one. The first two verbs (foreknew, predestined) refer back to God's eternal purpose. The next three verbs (called, justified, glorified) indicate the outworking in time of God's eternal plan.

8:26-30 Note the guarantees of glory: the action of the Holy Spirit (vv. 26-27), and the assurance of God's providence (vv. 28-30).

8:31-39 Note the great assurances: their relation to God (vv. 31b-33); their relation to Christ (v. 34); and their relation to circumstances (vv. 35-39).

8:33-34 It might be that our punctuation is faulty and that we preserve better the sweep of the text by understanding the last half of both verbs as rhetorical questions rather than statements. We would then translate, "Who will bring a charge against God's elect? God is the one who justifies" (The expected response to the question being, "Outrageous!" or "Of course not!"). "Who is the one who condemns? Christ Jesus is He who died . . . who was raised, who is at the right hand of God, who also intercedes for us?"

Translations and Interpretations for Consideration

8:28   "We know that in everything God works with those who love him, whom he has called in accordance with his purpose, to bring about what is good" (Goodspeed).

8:29   "For those whom he had marked out from the first he predestined to be made like his Son" (Goodspeed).

8:33   "Who shall impeach those whom God has chosen?" (Weymouth).

ROMANS 8:35-39   THE TRIUMPH OF FAITH

8:35   The rhetorical question, *"Who shall separate us from the love of Christ?"* may be converted to a strong assertion, "No one can separate us from Christ's love for us."

8:36   The quotation is from Psalm 44:22.

8:37   *"We overwhelmingly conquer."* This phrase translates the verb—a verb that occurs only here in the New Testament. Literally, it means to "super-conquer."

8:39   *"Nor any other* created thing." Paul adds this general phrase to cover all possible bases. There are two words translated "other" or "another" in our English translations. Here it means "another of different quality" and it is the word from which we get our English "heterodox." Paul wants to leave absolutely no room for doubt—nothing of any kind or description can separate the believer from the love of Christ.

Translations and Interpretations for Consideration

8:36   "We are being done to death for thy sake all day long" (NEB).

8:37   "Yet in all these things we keep on gloriously conquering through Him who loved us" (Williams).
       "But in all this He who loved us helps us win an overwhelming victory" (Beck).

ROMANS 9:1-33   GOD'S SOVEREIGNTY

9:1-33   How the gospel relates to Israel:
       The problem stated (vv. 1-5).
       The explanation offered (vv. 6-13).
       The objections answered (vv. 14-24).
       The proof given (vv. 25-29).
       The conclusion drawn (vv. 30-33).

9:1   Note the triple oathlike statement.
       "Bearing me witness." "Confidently assures me" or, more literally, "witnesses clearly."

9:3   *"Accursed."* We get our English word "anathema" from this term.

9:4-5   The eightfold privilege of Israel:

Adoption	Service of God
Glory	Promises
Covenants	Fathers (Patriarchs)
Giving of the law	Christ came in the flesh.

9:5   This verse has probably been discussed as much as any single verse in the New Testament. Punctuation is critical. The NASB and most translations very correctly punctuate in such a way as to refer the whole passage to Christ and strongly affirm His utter deity. Some commentators want a full stop in place of the comma and then a doxology directed toward God the Father.

"According to the flesh" is literally "as far as the flesh is concerned."

9:6-13 The Word of God had not failed (first proof, vv. 6-9; second proof, vv. 10-12). The Word of God is confirmed (v. 13).

9:8 *"Children of the flesh"* is not a reference to the manner of birth in contrast to caesarean section but means something like "physical descent."

9:9 Note Genesis 18:10.

9:11 *"Bad."* This is not the ordinary word for "evil" or "bad." The word more literally means "useless," thus highlighting the sovereignty of God.

9:12 Note Genesis 25:23.

9:13 Note Malachi 1:2-3.

Once again Paul makes an appeal to Scripture; this time to Malachi 1:2-3. The verb *"loved"* has the force of "chose," whereas the verb *"hated"* has the force of "rejected." In this type of context it seems particularly useful to employ such terms as "chose" and "rejected" rather than the literal *loved* and *hated*, especially since an equivalent of *hated* may give entirely wrong connotations in receptor language.[8]

9:14-18 Mercy comes according to divine will.

9:17 In this quotation God tells Pharaoh that He has two reasons for making him king: *"to demonstrate My power"* and *"that My name might be proclaimed throughout the whole earth."*

9:18 "Harden." The RSV and JB render this with the sense of "to harden [someone's] heart."

9:19-21 The divine right.

9:19 "Who resists His *will*?" The usual word for "will" or "desire" occurs sixty-four times in the New Testament. The word we have here occurs only here, in Acts 27:43, and 1 Peter 4:3. It is a stronger word indicating purpose and intent.

9:20 "But who are *you*, O man, who answers back to God?" The "you" is emphatic and is repeated. A word for word translation captures the force, *"You*, who are you to talk back to God?"

9:22-24 It seems that Paul does not complete his question but leaves it for the reader to supply something like, "Does he not act fairly?"

9:22　"Vessels of his wrath *prepared for destruction.*" The form of the participle could be either middle or passive, and what a difference it will make! If middle, they "have prepared themselves." If passive, they "have been prepared."

9:25　Note Hosea 1:9-10.

9:27　Note Isaiah 10:22-23.

9:29　Note Isaiah 1:9.

　　　The Scripture reference in this verse comes from the Septuagint of Isaiah 1:9. *"Lord Almighty"* is translated "Lord of Hosts" in most translations. This designation, frequently used in the Septuagint, means "Lord of the armies," a name which described the Lord's strength in battle. "The Lord who is all powerful," catches the gist of the phrase.

9:30-31　"The Gentiles, who did not pursue righteousness, have *attained* righteousness, even the righteous which is by faith; but Israel, pursuing a law of righteousness, did not *arrive* at that law." The KJV translates both verbs by "attained." The first verb means "to grasp" or "to seize," "to lay hold of as a prize." It is "attain" in the sense of arriving at a goal. The Gentiles seized the prize. The Jews pursued, but did not arrive at the goal.

9:30-33　Note the development: the question (vv. 30-31); the answer (v. 32*a*); the explanation (v. 32*b*); and the confirmation (v. 33).

9:33　Note Isaiah 28:16 and 1 Peter 2:8.

Translations and Interpretations for Consideration:

9:16　"So one's destiny does not depend upon his own willing or strenuous actions but on God's having mercy on him" (Williams).

ROMANS 10:1-21　　GOD'S RIGHTEOUSNESS

10:1　"My heart's *desire* and my *prayer* to God." The word "desire" is also used in the KJV and tends to be preserved in the major recent translations. Yet, strangely enough, that is not the precise meaning of the word as is clear from its use elsewhere in the New Testament. Ordinarily, it would be translated "good will' or "good pleasure." Perhaps its use here suggests the depth of affection imbedded in his desire for his people. The word translated "prayer" is one of several words for prayer in the New Testament. It is not a general word to cover all sorts of prayer, but rather suggests urgent petition. Likely it is the term which influenced the translators to render the former word as "desire."

10:2   In the phrase "in accordance with knowledge" the word for "knowledge" is a compound form and could be translated "true knowledge."

10:3   "For not knowing" translates one word in the Greek text, a present participle. We must not understand that the Jews had never heard about how God puts man right with Himself, but that they did not comprehend it.

10:4   "Christ is the end of the law." The word suggests something of both "fulfillment" and "termination."

10:5   Note Leviticus 18:5.

10:6-8 Quoting from Deuteronomy 30:12-14.

10:6   The phrase "to bring Christ down" does not suggest demoting Christ or removing him from his rightful position. It is speaking of his condescension on our behalf.

10:7   "The abyss." The NIV translates "the deep." The bottomless pit, the abode of the dead.

10:8   "The word of faith which we are preaching." How are we to understand this word? If it is an objective genitive, then it refers to the content of the proclaimed word. If it is subjective, then it indicates the response of faith to that proclaimed word. Here there is a definite article with the word faith ("the word of the faith") suggesting that it should be understood as objective.

10:9   "Jesus." From the Hebrew word, Joshua, meaning "Jehovah saves."

10:10   "For with the heart man believes." A mode of thinking, not feeling.
        "For with the heart man believes, resulting in righteousness, and with the mouth he confesses, resulting in salvation." The NIV has "you believe" and "you confess." Actually, the shift between verses 9 and 10 is in the voice of the verbs. A more literal translation is, "With the heart it (the gospel) is believed unto righteousness and with the mouth it (the gospel) is confessed unto salvation."

10:11   Note Isaiah 28:16 and Isaiah 49:23.
        The Scripture reference in this verse is to Isaiah 28:16 (see Romans 9:33).

10:11,13 Note the repetition of "whoever" in NASB.

10:12   "Abounding in riches." The NIV translates "richly blesses." A literal translation would be "is rich toward." Is generous to" or "gives good things to" would also be fair renderings.

10:13   Note Joel 2:32.
         In verse 13 Paul has affirmed that *"whoever will call upon
         the name of the Lord will be saved." The Lord* is Jesus
         Christ, and it is clear to Paul that the Jewish nation as a
         whole has not called upon the name of the Lord. In the
         remainder of this chapter Paul deals with the reasons for
         this unbelief.

10:15   The Scripture quotation in verse 15 comes from Isaiah 52:7.

10:16   See Isaiah 53:1.

10:17   The phrase *"word of Christ"* means "the message about
         Christ."

10:18   *"Surely they have never heard, have they?"* Compare the
         NIV here. "Did they not hear?" The NIV suggests the ex-
         pected answer is "yes" while the NASB anticipates a nega-
         tive reply. It is the same situation in verse 19. It seems that
         the dialogue becomes much more meaningful if you follow
         the NASB is this instance as normal Greek usage would
         anticipate the negative response.

10:19   Note Deuteronomy 32:21.
         "Israel did not know, did they?" In the Greek text the form of
         the question makes it clear that the expected answer to
         Paul's question, *"Did Israel not understand?"* is, "Yes, in-
         deed, they did know." Not only had they heard the message
         (v. 18), but they were capable of understanding it and hence
         were fully accountable to it.

10:20   Note Isaiah 65:1-2.

Translations and Interpretations for Consideration

10:2   "For I bear witness that they possess an enthusiasm for
         God, but it is an unenlightened enthusiasm" (Weymouth).

10:10   "With your heart you believe and and become righteous;
         with your mouth you confess and are saved" (Beck).
         "For with their minds men believe and are made upright,
         and with their lips they make the acknowledgment and are
         saved" (Goodspeed).

ROMANS 11:1-36   GOD'S FAITHFULNESS

11:1   "Did God reject *His people?"* A minor textual variant under-
         scores the utter impossibility posed by the question, for in
         place of "His people" it reads "His inheritance!"

11:2   *"Foreknew."* The word occurs seven times in the New Testa-
         ment. It means foreordination here and in Acts 2:23.

11:3   Note the *"altars,"* plural. Deuteronomy 12:13-14 makes it
         clear that there should never have been more than one.
         Hence Elijah's complaint.
         The passage quoted in verse 3 comes from 1 Kings 19:10, 14.
11:6   *"Of works"* does not constitute the basis for God's choice.
         One could translate, "For if God were to choose people on
         the basis of what they had done, then he wouldn't really be
         showing mercy."
11:7   *"Hardened."* The word means basically "covered with cal-
         louses."
11:8   *"To this very day"* is an expression found quite often in
         Deuteronomy and adds emphasis standing as it does as the
         final phrase in the sentence.
11:9   *"Table."* Refers to material prosperity.
         "Let their table become a *snare* and a *trap*, and a *stumbling
         block*." These are three words for "trap" and the overall
         picture seems to be that of taking wild birds.
11:12   "Their *failure* be riches for the Gentiles." The NIV translates
         "loss." The word is used only one other time in the New
         Testament, in 1 Corinthians 6:7, where the NIV translates it
         "defeat." The Jew's rejection of Christ was their defeat.
         The Greek word rendered *spiritual poverty* in the TEV is
         difficult to translate literally. Elsewhere in the New Testa-
         ment it occurs only in 1 Corinthians 6:7 with the meaning of
         "failure" or "defeat." The RSV renders the word by "failure"
         and the NEB by "falling-off." Goodspeed chooses the word
         "false step" and Moffatt "defection"; the JB translates by
         two words "fall and defection." Most commentators see in
         this word the meaning of "defeat," while others point out
         that the basic idea in this context is "smaller" or "less." If
         this last viewpoint is taken, the word may refer either to the
         small number of Jews who are saved or, as the TEV inter-
         prets it, to *their spiritual poverty*.[9]
         The meaning of the word "fulness" is disputed. It could be a
         reference to the time when the Jews will finally do the will
         of God (see Romans 13:10). Or it may indicate the complete
         number of Jews who will finally be included in God's salva-
         tion.
11:14   *"Move to jealousy my fellow countrymen"* is literally "make
         jealous my flesh." No doubt by "my flesh" Paul means his
         fellow Jews.
         "And save some of them." While a literal rendering of the

text may suggest that Paul himself is able to save some of them, we understand Paul's intent to be "because of what I have done God will save some of them."

11:16   It is quite likely, as many commentators point out, that both *"piece of the dough"* and *"root"* are references to the Jewish ancestors with whom God made his covenants. Paul is reminding the Gentiles that ultimately they owe their salvation to the Jewish people, for they owe their blessings to that spiritual root.

11:17-24 The parable of the olive tree: olives refer to Israel; wild olives refer to the Gentiles.

      Warnings for the Gentiles: against boasting (vv. 17-18); against being proud (vv. 19-21); and against being presumptuous (vv. 22-24).

11:17   *"If some of the branches were broken off."* This refers to the Dispersion in A.D. 70.

11:18   *"Do not be arrogant."* Perhaps "do not go on boasting" catches the flavor a bit better, particularly when we remember that Paul is writing to a Gentile church.

      In interpreting the term *"supports"* it is important to understand it as "nourishing" rather than "holding up." The sap flows from the root to the branches.

11:20   *"They were broken off for their unbelief."* Literally, "by unbelief they were broken off."

11:22-34 Note the comparisons. They are not as obvious in translation as in the Greek text: "cut out" as over against "cut in" (graft in); "by nature" versus "contrary to nature"; "a wild olive tree" (just one word in the Greek), "a cultivated olive tree" (one word), and "their own olive tree."

11:25   *"The fulness of the Gentiles."* The full number of Gentiles who will be saved. Note Acts 15:14.

      "Secret truth" is generally translated "mystery" (KJV, RSV, NAB), but several modern translators feel that this is inadequate. Moffatt and Goodspeed translate as "this secret," the JB as "a hidden reason," and the NEB as "a deep truth." This is a favorite Pauline expression, appearing some twenty-one times in his writings, and so it is important to give close attention to it. *Secret truth* or "mystery" was a very familiar term in the religious vocabulary of Paul's day. Each of the so-called "mystery religions" had a *secret truth* which was revealed only to the persons initiated into that particular religion. It was from this fact that the mystery

religions were so named. The same term frequently appeared in Jewish apocalyptic literature also, where it was
used to describe the *secret truth* of the way in which God
was at work in the world. And this was a truth which, of
course, was known only to God's faithful people. So both in
Judaism and in the other religions the term denoted a *secret
truth* which was once hidden but had not been revealed by
God to his people. It is in such a sense that Paul uses the
term in this passage and elsewhere.[10]

11:26   *"All Israel will be saved."* In context the reference must be to
the nation. Israel is to be saved as the crowning act of God's
mercy.

11:29   *"Irrevocable"* means "without change of mind or heart." It is
used in this sense in 2 Corinthians 7:10, its only other occurrence in the New Testament.

11:33   "How *unsearchable* are His judgments, and *unfathomable*
His ways!" The first word occurs only this time in the New
Testament and the second here and in Ephesians 3:8 where
it is translated "unsearchable."

11:36   *"From Him"* indicates that God is the source of everything.
"Through Him" indicates that God is the one who keeps the
created order in existence. He is the cohesive force in the
universe. *"To Him"* assures us that the created order is mov-
ing toward the goal he intends.
"Amen." Paul's response is, "This is surely true!"

Translations and Interpretations for Consideration

11:32   "For God has locked up all mankind in the prison of disobedience so as to have mercy on them all" (Williams).

11:34-35 "For who has ever understood the thoughts of the Lord, or
has ever been His advisor? Or who has ever advanced God
anything to have Him pay him back?" (Williams).

11:36   "For from Him everything comes; through Him everything
exists; and in him everything ends!" (Goodspeed).
"Source, Guide, and Goal of all that is—to Him be glory for
ever!" (NEB).

ROMANS 12:1-21   THE CHRISTIAN AND HIS MANNER OF LIFE

12:1   This is the *"therefore"* of consecration. See also the *"therefore"* of sanctification (Rom. 8:1), and the *"therefore"* of justification (Rom. 5:1).

"Holy." Set apart for God.

"By the mercies of God." These have been described in the preceding chapters.

See "What God Wants of You" in the devotional ideas section of this volume for treatment of this most significant verse.

12:2   *"Do not be conformed."* "Do not live according to the manner of this present age." The only other use of this Greek word is in 1 Peter 1:14.

"Renewing." A complete change for the better.

"Prove." Put to the test.

"Good, and acceptable and perfect." There is only one will of God, but we grow in our appreciation of that will from regarding it as good to the point where we regard it as perfect.

"Be able to test." See note on this word in Romans 1:28 and 2:18.

12:3   There is a beautiful play on words here. The root verb "to think" occurs no less than four times in this single verse. Twice it is the simple verb and twice it is in compound form. To catch the play on words one might translate, "Don't *think* grandly beyond what you ought to *think*, *think* so as to *think* straight."

12:3-8   See "Think Straight About Your Gifts" in the devotional ideas section of this book.

12:4   *"One body."* Note 1 Corinthians 12:12-31.

"The same function." The word from which we get *"praxis."*

12:6   *"Prophecy."* Forthtelling (1 Cor. 14:3).

"Since we have gifts . . . let us each exercise them accordingly: if prophecy, according to the proportion of his *faith.*" There is no word for "his" in the Greek text. Instead we have the definite article. Translating the phrase literally gives it quite a different thrust. The prophet is to prophesy according to *the* faith—that is, in faithfulness to the revelation once for all delivered to the saints. He does not do his own thing according to his own faith.

12:10   *"Be devoted to one another in brotherly love."* The verb in our English text reflects a noun which appears only here in the New Testament. The word suggests love within the family relationship.

12:11   *"Not lagging behind in diligence."* Literally, "Never be boiling over in spirit." The word "spirit" is taken by some as a reference to God's Spirit.

12:13a   *"Contributing to the needs of the saints."* The NIV is preferable to the NASB and KJV and reads: *"Share* with God's
people who are in need." "Sharing" is far more than contributing toward. But the Greek text may have a subtle over-
tone which would suggest "sharing the needs of the saints."
That is, sharing the needs of all the saints as an overall
habit. In other words, share the needs of all, not only those
who are peculiarly deprived.

12:13b   *"Practicing hospitality."* "Pursue" hospitality as a strenuous
and purposeful determination.

12:14   *"Bless."* "Eulogize." Literally, "to speak well of."

12:16   "Do not be haughty in mind, but *associate with the lowly."*
Since there is no word for "people" and since the form may
be either masculine or neuter, we should consider the possibility of translating something like, "adjust to com-
monplace affairs." There is a direct contrast in the verse
between "high things" and "humble things" or "humble
people." Either is possible.
Note Proverbs 3:7.

12:17   Note Proverbs 3:4.

12:19   *"Revenge."* To vindicate one's right.
"Leave room for the wrath of God." While this Greek text
has no word for "God," the context demands that we understand it to be God's wrath.
Note Deuteronomy 32:25.

Translations and Interpretations for Consideration

12:2   "Let your minds be remade and your whole nature thus
transformed" (NEB).

12:3   "Not to value himself unduly, but to cultivate sobriety of
judgment in accordance with the amount of faith which
God has allotted to each one" (Weymouth).

12:11   "Be thoroughly warm-hearted" (Weymouth).

12:12   "Maintain the spiritual glow" (Moffatt).
"Let hope keep you joyful; in trouble stand firm; persist in
prayer" (NEB).

12:13   "Share what you have with the holy people who need it"
(Beck).

ROMANS 13:1-14   THE CHRISTIAN AS A CITIZEN

13:1-2   "Let every person be *in subjection to* the governing au-
thorities. For there is no authority except from God, and

those which exist *are established* by God. Therefore he who *resists* authority has opposed the ordinance of God." An interesting fact concealed by our translations is that the italicized words are all forms of the same root verb, which means literally to "arrange in ranks." Thus, to submit is to line up in ranks under authority. To rebel is to line up in ranks against authority. To establish is to arrange matters firmly according to priority or rank.

13:1-4 Note that "God" is repeated five times in these four verses.

13:1 *"Let every person be in subjection."* The same Greek word as used in Titus 3:1 and in 1 Peter 2:13 where the individual's attitude toward the state is set forth.

"Every person" translates a Semitic idiom (literally "every soul"). Here, Paul expresses the normal Jewish attitude toward government.

13:2 *"Resists."* To arrange in battle formation in opposition.

13:4 *"Minister of God."* NIV translates "God's servant." A servant as seen in his activity.

"For it is a minister of God to you for good" is literally "for he is God's servant to you for good."

"For it does not bear the sword for nothing." "Sword" is a symbol of the government official's power to punish and the adverb "for nothing" must be taken to mean "without the power to use it."

13:6 "For because of this you also pay taxes." Compare the KJV "pay . . . tribute." Since in this instance the form of the imperative (command) is the same as that of the indicative (statement), the translator must make a choice.

13:7 *"Tax."* Personal property tax.
"Custom." "Toll."
"Fear." "Reverence."
"Tax" and *"custom."* It is difficult to distinguish between these two words. The first may be taken to refer to those taxes paid by a subject nation to a nation that is ruling it (see Luke 20:22), whereas the second word is a more general term that indicates taxes paid in support of a government (see Matt. 17:25). The first word may refer to direct taxes and the second to indirect taxes. However, Paul may intend no such subtle distinction.

The TEV translates those terms as "personal and property taxes," the JB as "direct tax or indirect." Perhaps some general phrase such as "taxes of any kind" would be more appropriate.

13:8a   *"Owe nothing to anyone."* The NIV nicely captures the flavor of the present tense. "Let no debt remain outstanding." This verse has been used as an argument against credit cards and mortgages, but verse 7 says, "Give everyone what you owe him" thus clearly indicating the Christian will have obligations. The point seems to be that he should pay what is due when it is due.

13:8b   "He who loves his *neighbor* has fulfilled the law." The words reflect an adjective meaning "another" or "other" and grammatically could either modify "law" or, as the NIV takes it — the direct object of the verbal form, "loves." In the first sense, "the one who loves has fulfilled the other law" — that is, the test of the law. Note how well this would go with the following verse.

13:8   *"Love."* This is a type of love like divine love (Gr. *agapaō*). Love is a debt.
         "Law." Some understand this to be a clear reference to the Jewish law, while others understand it to mean law in general. Since Paul quotes specific commands from the Old Testament, it seems better to take it as a reference to Mosaic law.

13:11   This verse is all one sentence in the Greek text.
         "Sleep." The NIV reads "slumber." This is the kind of sleep which one can never fully discharge. "Lethargy."
         "From sleep." "Out of your insensitivity to sin."
         "For now salvation is nearer to us than when we *believed*." The NIV has "first believed." While there is no word "first" in the Greek text, the verb "believed" is an aorist tense and must be taken as a reference to the time in the past when the Roman Christians first became believers.

13:12   *"Let us therefore lay aside the deeds of darkness."* Literally, "Let us put away the works of darkness." The tense of the verb suggests the initiation of an action, so "put aside" is appropriate. The "deeds of darkness" are the kind of things that one would do only in the dark.

13:13   *"Carousing and drunkenness."* Carousing ("orgies," NIV) is a very heavy word and is one which fits well with drunkenness. Interestingly enough, the word suggests excess in eating, which is one of the "nice" sins which we do not like to acknowledge. Note also that it stands first in the list.
         "Let us behave properly." Literally, "Let us walk becomingly." "Walk" in this sense is a Semitic term for "to live one's life."

13:14   *"Put on the Lord Jesus Christ."* Make Christ part of your daily life.
"Make no provision for the flesh." Deliberately avoid that which tempts you to sin.

Translations and Interpretations for Consideration

13:11   "We are now nearer being rescued than when we first believed" (Beck).
"In all this, remember how critical the moment is" (NEB).

13:13   "Let us behave with decency as befits the day" (NEB).

13:14   "Let Christ Jesus himself be the armour that you wear" (NEB).

ROMANS 14:1-23   CHRISTIAN LIBERTY AND CHARITY

14:1   *"One who is weak in faith."* One who does not yet have full knowledge of how to live as a Christian.
"Accept the one who is weak in *faith.*" The word "faith" here could be understood in either of two ways. It may indeed indicate the manner in which the brother is weak. It could, however, indicate the manner in which the weak brother is to be received — that is, *by faith.* Either is valid, and it might be that Paul was for this very reason purposefully ambiguous.

14:3   The verb *"regard with contempt"* is a very strong term. Paul is reminding his readers that God's acceptance of a person is based on his own grace and not on what a person does or does not do. Believers must accept one another in the same way.

14:4   *"Servant."* Household slave.
Who are you. . . ? The "you" stands first in the sentence and occurs again in the verb. A very literal translation might just capture the flavor. "You, who are you to judge someone else's servant?"

14:10   *"Judgment seat of God."* This is the Bema of God (2 Cor. 5:10).
The last part of this verse reads literally "for we shall all stand before the judgment seat of God." The purpose of this standing is clearly that we might be judged by Him.

14:11   Note Isaiah 45:23.
"It is written." (See Romans 1:17.) Once again Paul reinforces his argument by an appeal to Scripture. This time he quotes from Isaiah 49:18 and 45:23.

14:13   *"Stumbling block."* Temptation to sin.

"Judge." The NIV reads "passing judgment." Habitual criticizing of another.

"Therefore let us not *judge* one another anymore, but rather *determine this."* Since the italicized words translate the same word in the Greek text, the NASB may be preferable here.

This verb has already appeared five times in the earlier part of the chapter and has been translated "passing judgment on" in verse 1. In verse 4 it is translated "to judge." It is used (twice) in verse five where it is "regards." Its first use in this verse clearly means "to judge" or "to pass judgment on" and we understand it as a condemnatory judgment. The second instance suggests that the persons involved are to evaluate something and to make up their minds in regard to it.

14:14   *"Unclean."* This pertains to foods not permitted by the law (Lev. 11).

Note Mark 7:14-19.

"I know and am convinced" translates two verbs in the Greek text, the first meaning "know" and the second "persuade." The verbs are used to strengthen each other to the point of saying, "I am fully convinced" (NIV).

14:15   *"You are no longer walking according to love."* The verb "to walk in" has the same force here as in Romans 6:4; 8:4; and 13:13.

14:16   *"Good thing"* is ambiguous here. Is this a reference to Christian salvation? The plural "good things" is taken by TEV translators to have this meaning in Romans 10:15 where it is translated "good news." Or does the term "good things" relate to matters of Christian freedom? We cannot be certain.

14:17   *"Kingdom."* The present one, not the future one.

"Kingdom of God" is used only here in the book of Romans. The primary meaning of this phrase is always "the rule of God," the emphasis being upon the actual kingship or sovereignty of God rather than upon the territory of his kingdom.

In this context *"righteousness"* means "doing what God requires."

14:20   *"Do not tear down the work of God for the sake of food."* Recognizing the forensic nature of this letter and in view of the preceding discussion, it may be that we should not translate by a question but by a statement. To do so, usage will demand that it expect a negative answer. Hence, "You would not destroy the work of God for the sake of food, would you?"

14:21   *"It is good."* The English translation, unfortunately, does not enable us to see the play on words between the last part of verse 20 (Gr. *kakon*, "bad") and the first part of this verse (Gr. *kalon*, "good"). *The word could be translated "beautiful" or "attractive."*

14:22   *"Whatever you believe about these things."* A conviction or standard.

    "Happy." The NIV translates "blessed." Spiritually prosperous.

    "In what he approves." The word implies approval after thorough testing. See note on 2:18.

Translations and Interpretations for Consideration

14:1   "Treat people who are overscrupulous in their faith like brothers; do not criticize their views" (Goodspeed).

    "If a man is weak in his faith you must accept him without attempting to settle doubtful points" (Weymouth).

14:16   "Therefore do not let the boon which is yours in common be exposed to reproach" (Weymouth).

    "Your rights must not get a bad name" (Moffatt).

ROMANS 15:1-16:27   THE CHRISTIAN AS A WORKER

The concluding chapters of Romans present a number of interesting questions which scholars have debated through the centuries. For one thing Marcion omitted chapters 15 and 16 from his early edition. The grounds upon which he made his decision are unknown to us and a matter of great disagreement. For another, even the casual reader must note that there are three benedictions in these chapters. (At 15:33 we read, "The God of peace be with all of you. Amen." Again, at 16:20 we read, "The grace of our Lord Jesus be with you." Then, at the close comes the elaborate doxology of 16:25-27.) Each benediction provides a logical ending for the epistle and each has in fact been suggested as the original conclusion.

    Chapter 16 presents a variety of interesting questions in that it contains far more personal material than any other chapter in the New Testament. One theory is that this chapter was at any early date deleted as the epistle was widely circulated to churches which had no interest in the personal greetings.

15:1-3 Note the verb "to please" occurs in each of these verses. Use of that word in inscriptions suggests that it could bear the meaning of "serving in the interest of others" and may well have those overtones here.

15:1 *"Weaknesses."* Both physically and mentally.
"Ought." Under obligation.
"Strong." Morally strong (2 Cor. 13:9).
Note the pronoun "we." Paul includes himself among those who are "strong" in the faith.
"To bear" is the same verb used of Jesus carrying his cross in John 19:17 and of believers carrying their cross in Luke 14:27. This verb also occurs in Galatians 6:2. From its use elsewhere in the New Testament it is most likely that the verb means more than simply "to tolerate" or "to put up with." It may suggest that those who are strong in faith should be willing to suffer for the sake of those whose faith is weak.

15:2 *"Neighbor."* Since the passage is dealing with the Christian community, it is one's fellow Christian who is in focus.

15:3 The Scripture quoted is Psalm 69:9. In this one verse Paul appeals both to the example of Christ and the authority of the Scriptures—an appeal the early church would find compelling.

15:5 "May the God *who gives* perseverance and encouragement." Since there is no word in the Greek text behind the italicized, the KJV may make a good point in translating, "the God of patience and consolation." God, of course, does give these to His people, but the act of this giving flows from His very nature.

15:6 *"That."* In order that.
"With one accord you may with one voice." The NIV translates this phrase "one heart and mouth." Paul uses that phrase only here.
"Glorify." Keep on glorifying.

15:9 Note Psalm 18:49.
"I will give praise" is literally "I will confess to you" (see Rom. 14:11).

15:10 Note Deuteronomy 32:43.

15:11 This comes from Psalm 117:1. *"All you Gentiles"* and *"all the peoples"* are used synonymously in this verse. In Greek the

second imperative is a third person form (literally "let all
peoples praise him"), but in English the full force of the
form can only be expressed by means of a second person
imperative, "praise him, all peoples."

15:12   Note Isaiah 11:10.

15:13   *"In believing."* In the act of habitually believing.

"Fill you with all joy" may be rendered as "cause you to be
completely happy," "cause you to feel happy completely in
your hearts," or even "cause your hearts to burst because of
happiness." *Peace* also must be understood as the goal of
what God has caused: "that God may cause you to have
complete happiness and to enjoy peace" or "experience
complete peace." Peace may be expressed idiomatically in
some languages—for example, "to sit down in your hearts"
or "to hear quietness in your hearts."[11]

15:14   As is frequently the case, *"my brethren"* could well be rendered as "my fellow believers," or "you who are also follow-
ers of Christ."

"Admonish." "To give advice to" is used in a number of
translations. Paul is not thinking of formal teaching but of
the normal relationships within the Christian community.

15:16-20   Paul's ministry was very special: special message (v. 16);
special miracles (vv. 18-19); and a special method (v. 20).

15:16   *"To be a minister of Christ Jesus to the Gentiles, ministering
as a priest the gospel of God."* The word for "minister" here
is not the ordinary word which occurs many times in the
New Testament, and which has the very humble connotation of "servant," Rather, it is a rare word emphasizing the
dignity and value of the office. It is the word from which we
get the English word "liturgy." The participle behind the
phrase "with the priestly duty of" is likewise a high-
sounding word with professional liturgical overtones. It occurs only this time in the New Testament. Clearly, Paul is
concerned that the church at Rome know of the high dignity
of his office and work.

15:19   *"Signs."* This is one of seven Greek words used for miracles.
"Illyricum," Located on the eastern shore of the Adriatic. It
would be the present-day Yugoslavia.

"I have fully preached the gospel of Christ." There is nothing of "preach" in the Greek word. Rather, it means "fill up"
or "complete." Of course, we understand that proclamation
is involved. Paul regards his ministry in this vast area as
having been completely accomplished.

15:20   *"I aspired."* This expression conveys both the sense of earnest striving and the satisfaction derived from it.

15:23   *"No further place."* No more opportunity to preach Christ where He was unknown.

15:26   *"For Macedonia and Achaia have been pleased to make a contribution."* The phrase is almost an apologetic one— *some* offering. This is in marked contrast to the way in which Paul describes the giving of these people when he writes about them to the Corinthians. In 2 Corinthians 8, he praises them for generous and sacrificial giving to this cause. Could it be that the apostle anticipated (or even intended) that this letter to the church at Rome would find its way into the hands of the church in Jerusalem and now, for their eyes, speaks of this magnificent offering in rather apologetic terms? It is interesting that in this letter to a Gentile church which he has never seen, the apostle has more to say about the Jews (2:17f; 4; 9-11) than in any other of his letters and that he places the Jew in an extremely favorable light. Compare his letter to the Galatians on this score.

15:28   *"This fruit."* The money he was collecting.

15:30   *"I urge you, brethren, by our Lord Jesus Christ and by the love of the Spirit, to strive together with me in your prayers to God for me."* The "I urge you" is the same strong word of appeal that Paul used in 12:1. Obviously, this is something that Paul is tremendously burdened about. The phrase "strive together with me" translates a verb which occurs only this time in the New Testament. We get the English word "agony" from the root verb.

What was Paul so greatly concerned about? The following verse tells of two things: first, that the unbelievers in Judea might take his life; Second, that his "service" in Jerusalem "may be acceptable to the saints there." What does he mean by "service"? Surely it is the offering he is bringing (see vv. 25-27). Who ever heard of a preacher requesting prayer that an offering taken be accepted? Would accepting the offering imply full and complete recognition of Paul's apostolic authority and work by the church officials in Jerusalem? Would it also imply that this was the basis for his concern and request?

Translations and Interpretations for Consideration

15:1   "Those of us who have a robust conscience must accept as
        our own burden the tender scruples of weaker men, and not
        consider ourselves" (NEB).

15:13   "That you may bubble over with hope by the power of the
        Holy Spirit" (Williams).

ROMANS 16:1-27   GREETINGS TO THE SAINTS

Dr. A. Hayes, in his *Paul and His Epistles*, indicates that "The following facts have led to much questioning and discussion concerning
the last two chapters:

> In 1829 David Schulz made the suggestion that the sixteenth chapter
> with its very unusual number of personal salutations belonged not to
> the Epistle to the Romans, but to a copy of this epistle or some other
> epistle sent either by Paul or a Paulinist editor somewhere else, and
> most probably to Ephesus. This hypothesis has found favor with a
> great many modern critics. . . . The chief reasons for deciding that this
> chapter cannot belong to the Epistle to the Romans are:
> a) Paul is writing to strangers at Rome, but in this chapter he seems to
>   know all about the internal condition of the church with its dangers
>   from divisions and occasions of stumbling, and he seems to be
>   certain of the doctrine which has been taught to them.
> b) The number of salutations, 26 in all, points to a church in which
>   Paul was well acquainted, as the church in Ephesus, rather than to
>   one which he never had visited as the church in Rome.
> c) The persons greeted seem to belong to Ephesus rather than to Rome.
>   Aquila and Priscilla were at Ephesus a few months before Paul
>   wrote to the Romans, and in the next mention of them in the New
>   Testament, some eight or nine years later, they are still at Ephesus.
>   (1 Cor. 16:19; 2 Tim. 4:9).
> d) So many others mentioned here are Paul's kinsmen and fellow
>   workers, fellow prisoners and are his beloved friends, standing in
>   such relations of intimate fellowship and affection that we look for
>   them in a church where Paul had a long sojourn and had undergone
>   many perils.
> c) If all these good people were at Rome when Paul wrote this letter,
>   what became of them later?

Lightfoot, Lietzman, Cifford, Harnack, Sanday, Ramsay, Denney,
Codet, Zahn, Peake and others hold to the complete integrity of this
epistle."[12]

16:1   "*A servant* of the church which is at Cenchrea." More
        frequently than not the NIV renders this word "servant," as

it is here. It is the word from which we get our English word "deacon." The NIV does translate it "deacon" several times and on occasion, "minister." Clearly, the context demands that we see Phoebe as a leader in the church whether or not official office is to be understood.

The word "sister" (like the word "brother") is used in the sense of "fellow believer."

"Phoebe" is mentioned only here in the New Testament.

16:2   "She herself has also been a helper of many." The word behind our English translation is a word which occurs only here in the New Testament. It could be translated "defender" or "guardian" or perhaps even "legal representative." The word translated "leadership" by the NIV in Romans 12:8 is from the same root. Note that Phoebe has been this kind of help to Paul himself.

16:3   "Prisca and Aquila" are no doubt the two persons mentioned by name elsewhere in the New Testament.

16:5   "The church that is in their house." See 1 Corinthians 16:19; Colossians 4:15; and Philemon 2.

"Epaenetus" is mentioned only here in the New Testament. "Who is the first convert to Christ from Asia" is more literally "who is the firstfruit of Asia for Christ."

16:7   "Outstanding among the apostles." Well known to the apostles.

"Andronicus" and "Junias" are not mentioned elsewhere in the New Testament and may have been husband and wife or brother and sister.

16:7,   In those three verses we have the word "kinsman" or
11-12   "kinsmen." Is it likely that Paul would have so many relatives in this far-off church? The word could simply mean "Jews." The NIV understands it as such in 9:3 where it translates the word by phrase, "my own race." It could mean "of the same tribe." Perhaps all Jews in Tarsus as in other Greek cities were of the same tribe. Or it could, indeed, mean "relatives."

16:18   "Deceive." Beguile.

"Smooth . . . speech" translates a word which appears only here in the New Testament. It means something like "pleasant conversation."

"Minds" is literally "hearts." But in Semitic thought the heart was the seat of the intellect.

16:19 "I want you to be wise in what is good, and *innocent* in what is evil." The word more literally means "unmixed" and therefore "pure" or "uncontaminated."

16:20 *"The grace of our Lord Jesus be with you"* is a prayer to the end that "the Lord Jesus may act toward you in grace."

16:21 *"My relatives."* Not relatives, but fellow countrymen.

16:23 The name *"Gaius"* appears several times in the New Testament (Acts 19:29; 20:4; 1 Cor. 1:14; and 3 John 1.) Since it was a common name, it is doubtful that the same person is indicated in each case. Here Gaius is described as Paul's benefactor and the benefactor of the entire church. It would seem that Paul stayed in his home and that a house church met there.

16:24 Many manuscripts do not contain this verse.

16:25 *"Kept secret."* To be kept in silence.
"Mystery." Something unknown in times past but revealed in the New Testament.
"My gospel." See note on Romans 1:1b.

16:26 *"But now is manifested, and by the Scriptures of the prophets."* With the strong emphasis on "now," the "prophetic writings" would seem to be the New Testament Scriptures.

Translations and Interpretations for Consideration

16:16 "Greet one another with the kiss of peace" (NEB).

16:19 "But I wish you to be wise as to what is good, and simple-minded as to what is evil" (Weymouth).

16:19 "Yet I should wish you to be experts in goodness but simpletons in evil" (NEB).

NOTES

1. C. H. Dodd, *The Epistle to the Romans* (New York: Harper & Row, 1932), p. 8.
2. Frederic W. Farrar, *The Life and Work of St. Paul* (Minneapolis: Klock & Klock Christian Publications, 1980), p. 459.
3. Barclay M. Newman and Eugene A. Nida, *A Translator's Handbook on Paul's Letter to the Romans* (London: United Bible Societies, 1973), p. 44.
4. Ibid., p. 93.
5. Ibid., p. 119.
6. Ibid., p. 133.
7. Ibid., p. 133.
8. Ibid., p. 184.
9. Ibid., p. 215.
10. Ibid., p. 225.
11. Ibid., p. 277.
12. D. A. Hayes, *Paul and His Epistles* (New York: Methodist Book Concern, 1915), p. 323.

Certain it is that no book has had a greater influence on the theology of the Protestant Church, and no book contains more of the quintessence of the mind of Paul. It is not an easy book to understand, for Paul is leading men in it into the deep things of the Christian faith, and he is often writing at such white-heat that the threads of his words are difficult to disentangle.[1]

William Barclay

6

Doctrinal Study

Although Romans was written in the form of a letter, no other book of the New Testament with the exception of the epistle to the Hebrews approaches so nearly the character of a doctrinal treatise. In no other letter is Paul so free of local and specific concerns and consequently so able to share in closely reasoned fashion the distilled and carefully formulated fruit of his thought.

For the purpose of systematic theology, Romans is the most important book of the Bible as Paul, much like a systematic theologian, reflects more briefly on those truths about which he had written in his earlier letters (often in the nature of a concise comment on a current situation or problem).

Students of historic theology may trace the influence of the book of Romans down through the centuries, as it has had a dominant impact in forming the dogma of the Christian church from its beginning to the present day.

Although it does not contain a complete statement of Christian doctrine (having no special emphasis on Christology as do Colossians and Ephesians, and no teaching about eschatology as does Thessalonians), it does deal with a number of great theological principles in a thoroughly comprehensive way. Themes such as sin, righteousness, grace, law, justice, and love are dealt with in great depth and call our attention to the profound theological importance of the epistle.

It can be safely said that no other book is so significant for the study of Christian doctrine.

THE DOCTRINE OF GOD IN ROMANS

SUMMARY

The epistle to the Romans sets forth God as creator, judge, and ruler of this world. As the creator of all that exists, He is of necessity everlasting and uncorruptible. His creation also bears witness of His infinite power and total foreknowledge.

God is the judge and ruler of the world. Happily, His judgments are righteous, unsearchable, and sure. He who rules the world is utterly wise, scrupulously fair, infinitely loving, and good. Hence, the righteous need not fear His judgments.

The God who is the creator delights to act as a Father toward all who come to Him through faith in His Son, Jesus Christ. The Holy God made provision to justify sinful man by sending His only begotten Son as a propitiation for man's sins in order that men might be reconciled to God. We must face the fact that wrath and justice are among God's attributes. The good news is that God's wrath will be manifested only upon those who refuse to recognize His love and appropriate His provision for sin.

God, who is all-wise and who alone rules the world, has provided a spiritual kingdom where those who desire to follow Him may do so as His servants, His heirs, and ones possessing eternal life.

More clearly than any other book in the Bible, Romans declares that the infinite God has revealed Himself to man through His creation, through man's conscience, through the Scriptures, and most clearly, through His Son Jesus Christ.

SURVEY

Attributes:

1:10; 8:27; 12:2; 15:32	Will
1:16	Powerful
1:17; 3:5, 22	Righteous
1:18	Wrathful
1:23; 3:23; 5:2; 15:7	Glorious
1:25; 3:4; 15:8	Truth
16:27	Wisdom
2:4; 11:22	Goodness
2:13	Justice
3:18	Fearful
3:25	Forbearance
3:30	One
5:5-8; 8:39	Love
11:33	Knowledge
16:26	Eternal

Approach:

1:8; 7:27	In Christ
5:2	By faith
8:17	Through Holy Spirit
10:1; 15:30	With prayer
15:6	To glorify Him

Nature of God:

1:7	Father
1:20	God
1:25	Creator
1:32	Lawgiver
3:25	Redeemer
9:18	Sovereign
14:10-12	Judge
14:17	King

Christian and God:

1:7	Beloved
3:23	Sinner saved by grace
4:3	Believed God
4:20; 15:6	Give glory to God
5:1	Peace with God
5:5	Love of God in hearts
5:11	Joy in God
6:10-11	Live unto God
6:13	Yielded to God
6:22	Servants
7:11	Bear fruit
7:25	Serve the law of God
8:1	No condemnation
8:21	Liberty
8:28	Love God
8:30; 11:2	Foreknowledge
8:31; 9:18; 12:3	Sovereign
9:5	Blessed
9:11	Purposeful
9:16; 12:1; 15:9	Merciful
9:22	Longsuffering
10:2	Zealous

11:22	Severity
12:1	Living sacrifices
14:12	Give account
15:5	Patience
15:13	Hope
15:33; 16:20	Peace

Revealed through:

1:1	Gospel
1:8	Christ
1:20	Nature
2:15	Conscience
3:21; 10:17	Scriptures

Judgments of God:

2:2; 3:6	According to truth
2:2	Against evil
2:3	Inescapable
2:5	Righteous
2:16	Open and searching
3:18-19	Just, upon the guilty
11:33	Unsearchable
14:11-12	All are subject to Him

Works of God:

1:9	Witness to believer
2:29	Praise the believer
3:2	Gave the law
3:25	Sent Son to be propitiation
4:6	Imputes righteousness
4:17	Quickens the dead
4:20	Giver of promises
5:10	Reconciles sinners
6:23	Gives gift of eternal life
8:3	Sent His Son
8:32	Give us all things in Christ
8:33	Justifies
9:16	Shows mercy
10:1; 15:30	Hears prayer
10:9	Raised Jesus from the dead
11:21	Spared not the natural branches

THE DOCTRINE OF CHRIST IN ROMANS

SUMMARY

The epistle to the Romans is particularly rich in Christology. Not only are the great facts of Christ's life that serve as a foundation for the gospel highlighted (His death, resurrection, and ascension), but the works of Christ are also highlighted. In this letter as nowhere else in the New Testament we find the motif of Christ as the second Adam. Also distinctive of this letter is the forensic emphasis on Christ as ransom and substitute.

God raised His only Son from the dead to demonstrate that He is the Son of God. As the eternal Son of God, our Lord is fully qualified to represent God to man. In Romans we see Him at the right hand of God dispensing justice.

As the One who was born of the seed of David according to the flesh (a Jew), He partook of our humanity and so is able to represent man to God. As God's provision for man's atonement, He died for sin in order that He might redeem man, and that man might enjoy eternal life and peace with God.

In Christ the believer is a joint heir with Christ, and hence, the recipient of the riches of God's love and kingdom.

Because He is truly God and truly man, our Lord is our one and only Mediator and is uniquely qualified to serve as man's final Judge.

SURVEY

Death of Christ:

3:25-26	Obedience to law's demands (propitiation)
3:26	Redeemed
4:25	Ransom paid for our freedom
5:6-8	Substitute for sinner
5:8	Assurance of love of God
5:10-11	Reconciled to God

Resurrection of Christ:

4:25; 6:4, 9; 10:6-7	Our justification
16:5	Our firstfruits

Ascension of Christ:

8:34	Arrived in heaven
8:34	At right hand of Father
12:3-8	High priestly work today: bestows spiritual gifts

Works of Christ:

2:16; 14:10	Judge
3:24; 4:25; 5:10-11, 15	Redeemer
4:25	Justifier
5:6-8; 8:34; 14:9	Died for us
5:8	Substitute
6:4, 9	Resurrection
8:9-11	Indweller
8:34	Intercessor
10:4	Fulfiller of the law

Gifts of Christ:

1:7; 5:1	Peace
1:7; 5:15; 16:20, 24	Grace
1:16	Gospel—not ashamed
3:22; 5:17	Righteousness
5:21; 6:23	Eternal life
15:19; 16:25	Gospel—fully preached
15:29	Gospel—blessings

Humanity of Christ:

1:3	Seed of David
6:4, 9	Raised from the dead
1:3; 9:5	Came in flesh
15:8	Minister to the circumcision

Christian's Relationship to Christ:

1:1; 14:18	Servant
1:6	Called
1:8; 7:25	Thanks be to Christ
1:16	Power
5:11	Joy in God through Christ

6:3	Baptized
6:8-11	Alive in Christ
8:1	No condemnation
8:2	Freedom from law of sin and death
8:17	Joint heir
8:34, 39	Love of Christ always
12:5	One body
13:14	Put on Christ
14:15	Mutual love
15:17; 16:27	Glory through Christ
15:20	New ministry
16:3	Helper
16:9-10	In Christ
16:16	Fellowship with believers

Christ's Relationship to God:

1:4; 1:9; 5:10	Son of God
2:16	Administrator of God's justice
3:25	God's sacrifice of atonement
5:15-17	The gift from God
8:11; 1:4; 4:24; 5:10; 6:4-5; 10:9	God raised Him from the dead
8:34	He is at the right hand of God

Christ's Relationship to Man:

1:3	Born according to the flesh Born of the seed of David
2:16	He is to be our judge
3:24-25; 4:25; 5:10-11, 15	He is our redeemer
3:25; 4:25; 5:6; 5:10; 8:34	He died for our sins
4:25	He is our justifier
5:1	Man has peace with God through Jesus Christ
5:8	He is our substitute
5:9	Christ was man's redeemer

6:3, 5; 8:17, 32	There is a union between man and Christ
6:23	Man has eternal life through Christ
8:17	Man is a joint heir with Christ
8:34	He is our intercessor

The Results Brought About Through the Mediator:

5:1	He gave us peace
5:11	We have received the atonement through Christ
5:17	He gave us a righteousness
6:4	Christ is our pattern
6:23; 5:21	He gave us eternal life
8:1	There is no condemnation to those in Christ Jesus
8:2	He freed us from sin Free from the law of sin and death
8:4	That the righteousness of the law might be fulfilled in us
8:35	He takes us back to God

THE DOCTRINE OF THE HOLY SPIRIT IN ROMANS

SUMMARY

The epistle to the Romans is exceedingly rich in terms of teaching concerning the third member of the Trinity, the Holy Spirit. Romans 8, frequently designated "the chapter of Christian victory," could as well be called "the chapter on the Holy Spirit." The Spirit is referred to as "the spirit of holiness" (1:4), "the Spirit of life" (8:2), "the Spirit of God" (8:14), and "the spirit of adoption" (8:15).

Central to the teaching of the book is the fact that the believer lives in the realm of the Spirit. Throughout the book the sphere of the Spirit is contrasted with the sphere of the flesh. The quality of life in the Spirit is radically different from that of life in the flesh. It is by the Spirit that we become children of God in the first place. As that Spirit of life or Spirit of God is allowed to permeate the believer's life, the believer is sanctified through Him as the new Spirit puts to death the fleshly deeds of the body.

The final, glorious result of the presence of the Holy Spirit in one's life is that our mortal bodies will be transformed. Thus, the Holy Spirit, who operates daily in the believer's body to produce the fruit of the Spirit and to minister to his weakness, will ultimately transform the body itself.

SURVEY

Attributes:

5:5; 15:30	Love
8:2, 10, 13	Life
8:9-11	Personality
15:13, 19	Power

Christian and the Holy Spirit:

5:5	Love of God shed in hearts
8:4	Walk after the Spirit
8:5	Mind the things of the Spirit
8:6	Peace in the Spirit
8:9, 11	Indwells
8:11	Quickened by the Spirit
8:14	Deeds of the body put to death
	Spirit leads
8:16	Spirit bears witness
8:23	Firstfruit
8:26-27	Prayer
8:27	Searches our hearts
15:16	Sanctification
	Righteousness in the Spirit

Note: Romans 8 contains all but six references to the Holy Spirit in the book of Romans.

THE DOCTRINE OF SALVATION IN ROMANS

SUMMARY

Instruction concerning salvation is what the book of Romans is all about. The early chapters show the depth of man's need for salvation. Then Paul proceeds to show not only the provision of salvation for all, but goes to great pains to make clear just what salvation really is. In the final chapters Paul teaches us what the fruits of salvation are.

Strangely enough, the words "salvation" and "saved" do not occur with great frequency. Paul rather prefers other terms such as "justification" and "justify" or phrases such as "to make righteous" or "bestow righteousness" to describe the salvation experience. Redemption, grace, adoption, and imputation are all concepts developed in Romans. Each gives vital insights into the salvation work wrought by our Lord. Taken together they describe the full-orbed beauty of the believer's salvation.

Salvation is the free gift of God granted to all who believe in their hearts and confess with their mouths that Jesus is Lord.

Throughout the epistle we sense the great desire of the apostle that all men everywhere, Jew and Gentile alike, avail themselves of the marvelous salvation he so carefully delineates in his letter.

SURVEY

1:16	The gospel is the means of salvation
2:7	We need to continue in well doing
3:22	Salvation is given to all through belief in Jesus Christ
5:9-10	We are justified by His blood; saved from wrath; saved by His life
5:1	We have peace
5:5	God's love—shed by the Holy Spirit
5:11	We have joy in God
6:4	A freshness of life
6:22	Freed from sin—and everlasting life
6:23	Salvation is a free gift
8:24	Saved by hope; 8:29-30— election has a part
10:1	Paul desired Israel's salvation
10:6-8	This salvation is ever near us
10:9-10	We must confess and believe
11:11	Israel's fall brought salvation to the Gentiles
12:1-2	Consecration is needed
13:11	Now is the time of salvation

THE DOCTRINE OF SIN IN ROMANS

SUMMARY

Romans has more to say about sin than any other book in the Bible. It speaks of the origin of sin, the nature of sin, the results of sin, the universality of sin, the dominion of sin, man's struggle with sin, and the remedy for sin.

The bad news is that all have sinned. As long as we live in this world, sin remains our problem and our enemy.

Sin is rebellion against a holy God and must be punished by God. Christ bore the punishment for us so that we might be saved.

Death is the inevitable result of sin. Life is the certain result of faith in Christ.

Sin entered the world through one man, Adam, and corrupted all his descendants. Provision for man's sin was made by the man Christ Jesus and is freely bestowed upon each one of His spiritual descendants.

The good news is the victory over sin is available to all in Christ!

SURVEY

2:12-13	They who have sinned in the law shall be judged by the law
3:7	Sin hinders God, thus it is punishable
3:8	Do not sin in order that grace may abound
3:9	Jews and Gentiles are both under sin
3:12, 23	All have sinned
3:20	For by the law is the knowledge of sin
3:25	Blood shed for the remission of sins
4:8	Blessed is the man to whom the Lord will not impute sin
4:15	No sin without the law
5:8	We were sinners at the time Christ died for us
5:12	By one man sin entered into the world, and death by sin
5:13	For until the law sin was in the world: but sin is not imputed when there is no law

5:19	By Adam's disobedience many were made sinners
5:20	Where sin abounded, grace did much more abound
5:21	Sin has reigned unto death
6:1	Shall we continue in sin that grace may abound?
6:2	How shall we, who are dead to sin, live any longer in it?
6:6	That the body of sin might be destroyed
6:7	He who is dead is freed from sin
6:10	For in that he died, he died unto sin once
6:11	Reckon also yourselves to be dead indeed unto sin
6:12	Let not sin reign in your mortal body
6:13	Neither yield your members as instruments of unrighteousness unto sin
6:14	For sin shall not have dominion over you
6:15	Shall we sin because we are not under the law?
6:16	Whether of sin unto death or obedience unto righteousness
6:17	But God be thanked, that you became obedient
6:18	Being then made free from sin
6:20	For when you were the servants of sin
6:22	But now being made free from sin
6:23	For the wages of sin is death
7:7	Is the law sin? God forbid.
7:8	But sin, taking occasion by the commandment
7:9	But when the commandment came, sin revived, and I died
7:11	For sin, taking occasion by the commandment, deceived me

7:13	But sin, that it might appear sin, working death in me by that which is good; that sin by the commandment might become exceeding sinful
7:14	But I am carnal, sold under sin
7:17, 20	Sin that dwells in me
7:23	Bringing me into captivity to the law of sin that is in my members
7:25	But with the flesh the law of sin
8:2	For the law of the Spirit of life in Christ Jesus has made me free from the law of sin and death
8:3	He condemned sin in the flesh
8:10	The body is dead because of sin
11:26	Christ shall turn away sin from the Jews
12:9	Abhor evil
12:17	Return not evil for evil
13:3	Rulers frighten the evildoers
14:20	It is evil for that man who eats and gives offense
14:23	For whatsoever is not of faith is sin

THE DOCTRINE OF GRACE IN ROMANS

SUMMARY

Grace is a significant word in the salutation and, if your Bible translation includes verse 24 of chapter 16, there is a beautiful benediction of grace just preceding the closing words of the letter. Every argument of the book and every theme introduced relates to grace, either by contrast or by association.

Paul showed that man is a sinner only to demonstrate that where sin abounded grace did much more abound. Justification, sanctification, election, the law, and faith are all set forth in a context of the sovereign grace of God.

Grace is the unmerited favor which flows from a holy God to the sinner, justifying him and making him acceptable to God. All of the gifts the believer enjoys from the hand of God are gifts of His grace. In addition to those general gifts of grace which every believer ought to enjoy, there are individual gifts of grace for all who believe.

SURVEY

1:5	By whom we have received grace and apostleship
1:7	Grace to you and peace from God our Father
3:24	Being justified freely by His grace
4:4	Now to him that works is the reward not reckoned of grace
4:16	It is of faith, that it might be by grace
5:2	By whom also we have access by faith into this grace wherein we stand
5:15	Much more the grace of God
5:17	Much more they which receive abundance of grace
5:20	Where sin abounded, grace did much more abound
5:21	Even so might grace reign through righteousness
6:1	Shall we continue in sin that grace may abound?
6:14	For you are not under the law, but under grace
6:15	Because we are not under the law, but under grace
11:5	Even so then at this present time also there is a remnant according to the election of grace
11:6	If by grace, then is it no more of works: otherwise grace is no more grace. But if it be of works, then is it no more grace.
12:3	Through the grace given unto me

12:6	Having then gifts differing according to the grace that is given to us
15:15	Because of the grace that is given to me of God
16:20	The grace of our Lord Jesus Christ be with you
16:24	The grace of our Lord Jesus Christ be with you all

THE DOCTRINE OF FAITH IN ROMANS

SUMMARY

On the human side, faith is the means by which grace and all that accompanies it becomes operative in the believer's life. Without a personal faith or trust in Jesus Christ there is no salvation, justification, or redemption as far as the individual is concerned. We must understand that New Testament faith is far more than intellectual assent. It is, as well, a matter of heart commitment.

In this letter Paul dealt at length with the principles of faith and law, showing that faith is not contrary to the law, but when rightly understood, establishes the law. He demonstrated that Israel's failure was in large measure due to their boasting in the law rather than recognizing that without faith the works of the law are void.

1:5	For obedience to the faith among all nations
1:8	That your faith is spoken of throughout the whole world
1:12	That I may be comforted together with you by the mutual faith
1:17	For therein is the righteousness of God revealed from faith to faith: as it is written, the just shall live by faith
3:3	Shall their unbelief make the faith of God without effect?
3:22	Even the righteousness of God which is by faith in Jesus Christ
3:25	Whom God hath set forth to be a propitiation through faith in his blood

3:27	But by the law of faith
3:28	We conclude that a man is justified by faith without the deeds of the law
3:30	Which shall justify the circumcision by faith and uncircumcision through faith
3:31	Do we then make void the law through faith
4:5	His faith is counted for righteousness
4:9	For we say that faith was reckoned to Abraham for righteousness
4:11	A seal of the righteousness of the faith
4:12	Who also walk in the steps of that faith of our father Abraham
4:13	Through the righteousness of faith
4:14	Faith is made void
4:16	It is of faith . . . which is of the faith of Abraham
4:19	Being not weak in faith
4:20	But was strong in faith, giving glory to God
5:1	Therefore being justified by faith
5:2	By whom also we have access by faith
9:30	Even the righteousness which is of faith
9:32	Because they sought it not by faith
10:6	But the righteousness which is of faith
10:8	The word of faith which we preach
10:17	So then faith coming by hearing
11:20	You stand by faith
12:3	According as God hath dealt to every man the measure of faith
12:6	Let us prophesy according to the proportion of faith

14:1	Him who is weak in the faith receive
14:22	Have you faith?
14:23	He eats not from faith: for whatsoever is not from faith is sin
16:26	Made known to all nations for the obedience of faith

THE DOCTRINE OF THE CHURCH IN ROMANS

SUMMARY

There is no doubt that the letter to Rome was addressed to the Christian community—that is, to all those in Rome who were called saints. From the concluding chapter it is evident that there were several house churches within the city.

The church was an exceedingly important concept to the apostle Paul, and he wished the Christians at Rome to share it. In the concluding chapter not only did he greet the church at Rome from the church at Corinth where he was located at the time of writing, but also from "all the churches of Christ."

Paul was concerned for the unity of the church in Rome and urged them to avoid factions. He was concerned for the spiritual maturity and commitment of the church and urged them to present themselves to God. Also of concern to Paul was that the gifts given the church be properly used. All of that is in relation to a church Paul himself had not yet seen and whose specific needs and problems he did not know!

SURVEY

Local Church:

16:1	Servants
16:2	Members
16:4	Of Gentiles
16:5	In homes
16:23	Hosting the whole church
1:7	Beloved God

Church (the Body):

1:12	Mutual faith
6:3	Identified with Christ totally
6:14	Not under law, but under grace

12:1	Sacrifice, living
12:5	One Body
12:6-8	Spiritual gifts given
12:9	Love in the Body

THE DOCTRINE OF LAW IN ROMANS

SUMMARY

One of the exceedingly important concepts in the book of Romans is that of the law of God. The word "law" occurs with great frequency in the book. The reader soon understands that the word is not always used in the same sense. It is utterly important to stop and ask just what did Paul mean by "law" in the passage before me? Sometimes he meant the Old Testament law. At other times he meant the moral law that is written into the heart of His creation.

Also, it is evident from the epistle that law serves many functions. The law reveals man's transgression. The law motivates man to righteous living. The law demonstrates the folly of man's effort to be saved by his own lawkeeping. The works of the law are set in sharp contrast to God's provision of grace.

SURVEY

Sin and the Law:

2:12	Perish without the law
2:23	Breaking the law
3:20; 7:8	Knowledge of sin
5:13	Sin is imputed
7:12	The law is holy
7:16	The law is good
7:14	The law is spiritual
7:23	Captivity to law of sin
8:2	Death
9:31; 10:5	Not attained the law of righteousness

Instruction:

2:18	Out of the law
2:20	Truth in the law
3:19	Under the law
3:21	Of God's righteousness
3:31	Established

Justification:

2:13	Doers of the law
2:17	Rests in the law
3:27	Law of faith; law of commandments
3:28	By faith without the deeds of the law
6:14-15	Not under the law but under grace
7:1-6	Dead to the law by the body of Christ
7:22	Law of God after the inward man
8:2-8	Law of the Spirit of life

Judgment:

2:12	By the law
4:15	Law works wrath

Additional References:

2:14-15	7:25
2:25	9:4
2:27	10:4
5:20	13:8
7:7	13:10
7:9	

THE DOCTRINE OF ISRAEL IN ROMANS

SUMMARY

Paul the apostle to the Gentiles had more to say about the Jew in his letter to the Roman church than he did in any other letter. He points out the great advantages the Jews have enjoyed and makes certain that the Gentiles are aware of their great indebtedness to the Jew. In no other New Testament book is the Jew pictured in such a favorable light.

To whom much is given, from him much will be required. Paul made it very clear that the Jew is guilty before God for refusing the salvation of God in spite of his many advantages.

Yet, God has not forgotten His earthly people. Not only are believing Jews incorporated into the Body of Christ along with believing Gentiles, but Paul makes it plain that there is a very special place for the Jew in the future. The validity of God's opening the door of salvation to the Gentiles rests in the fact that God is very faithful in keeping His promise to His earthly people.

SURVEY

1:16	The Jew was given the first chance to be saved
2:9	Anguish of soul upon the Jew first
2:17	The Jews were confident in the law
2:24	Their unfaithfulness is affecting the Gentiles
3:9	For we have before proved both Jews and Gentiles
3:29	Is He the God of the Jews only?
9:6	For they are not all Israel, which are of Israel
9:24	Whom He has called, not of the Jews only
9:27	Isaiah also cries concerning Israel
9:31	But Israel, which followed after the law of righteousness
9:32	The Jews missed Christ by paying too much attention to the Law
10:1	My heart's desire and prayer to God for Israel is salvation
10:2-7	Over zealous, spiritual ignorance, and egotism
10:18	They have heard of the way of salvation
10:19	Did not Israel know?
10:21	But to Israel he says
11:2	How he makes intercession to God against Israel
11:5	They are the objects of election
11:7	Israel has not obtained what she seeks for
11:11	Through their fall, salvation came to the Gentiles
11:23-24	They have the possibility of a future restoration
11:25	That blindness in part is happened to Israel

11:26	And so all Israel shall be saved
11:28	They are the recipients of God's love

THE DOCTRINE OF THE GENTILES IN ROMANS

SUMMARY

Paul, the great apostle of the Gentiles, informed the church in Rome that he had a great desire to visit them and have a harvest among them just as he had among *other* Gentiles. Although there was a strong Jewish contingency, it seems that the church in Rome was predominantly Gentile.

In the early part of the epistle Paul makes it clear that as Gentiles they are guilty before God since they have not lived up to the light that God had given them and because they had failed to recognize and worship the God of creation. As in no other letter he paints a dark picture of the sin and perversity of the Gentile world.

The heart of the epistle is designed to show that as Gentiles they are recipients of the full and free grace of God as manifested in Jesus Christ and, along with the Jews, are candidates for salvation. Since the Jew failed in his responsibility to be a light to the Gentile, the gospel now flows directly to the Gentile on an equal basis with the Jew.

Nevertheless, Paul made it clear that the Gentile must not despise the Jew. Rather, he must recognize the great debt he owes to the Jew as, most important of all, it was through the Jew that the Scriptures and the Savior came.

SURVEY

Ministry to:

1:13	Fruitful
3:30	Through faith
2:26; 9:30; 15:27	Attained faith
11:11	Salvation results
11:13; 15:16	Their apostle, Paul
11:25	Fullness of times (Gentile)
15:12	In Christ shall they trust
15:18	Obedient by word and deed
16:4	Churches of the Gentiles arise

Gentiles Themselves:

2:9	Do evil
2:24	Blaspheme
3:9	Under sin
9:24	Prepared unto glory
15:9	Glorify God for His mercy
15:10	Rejoice

Jew and Gentile:

2:10	Common benefits: glory, honor, peace
3:29	Common belief: God

Additional References:

1:16
2:14
15:11
15:18

DEFINING SIGNIFICANT DOCTRINAL WORDS IN ROMANS

We say that we believe the Bible to be the very Word of the living God. We affirm that the inspiration of Scripture extends to the very choice of the words by the author. Or, to put it differently, we say that we believe in the verbal inspiration of Scripture. If we really believe that, then obviously every word is important. One of the best ways to study the Bible is to study the individual words. The following are some of the key words in Romans. (Please note that all statistics refer to occurrences in the Greek text.)

Adoption. Here is a significant word used only by Paul in the New Testament. Two of the five times it occurs are in Romans and it means literally "to be established as a son." It is the receiving into a family of one who does not belong to it by birth.

Apostle. The noun occurs three times and literally means "a sent one." The verb occurs once (10:15) and means "to send."

Baptism. The meaning is "to dip or immerse." The word is used only once in Romans (6:4).

Blood. Of ninety-six occurrences in the New Testament only three are in Romans, two of which (3:25 and 5:9) have theological significance. By "blood" here, we understand Christ's sacrifice on our behalf.

Called. Occurring four times in Romans, Paul's usage of the word invariably indicates something of God's intention and design for the person or persons involved. Thus, Paul was "designated" an apostle and the believer a saint.

Concepts. In addition to single words, there are concepts Paul uses in writing to the Romans that we should note with particular care, such as "wrath of God," "will of God," "fear of God," "love of God," "oracles of God," and "righteousness of God." Although the exact phrases do not occur with great frequency, the concepts appear in a variety of expressions and are exceedingly important to the argument of the book. Then, too, there are words that occur in almost every sentence such as "God," which occurs 153 times; "Christ," which occurs sixty-seven times; the phrase "in Christ," twelve times; and the word "law," seventy-one times.

Condemnation. Under "judgment" we note that that word could mean a negative judgment or condemnation. But this is a stronger word, which occurs three times in Romans (5:16, 18; 8:1) and nowhere else in the New Testament, and definitely means a harsh or condemnatory judgment.

Death. The word is used twenty-four times in this epistle and is related to the verb "to kill." It is used with various nuances in this letter, but one way or another suggests the idea of separation (6:2).

Debtor. This is "one who owes." Of seven times in the New Testament, it occurs three times in Romans (1:14; 8:12; 15:27).

Faith and *Believe.* Since the noun "faith" and the verb "to believe" are from the same stem, they should be considered together. The noun occurs thirty-seven times in Romans and the verb twenty-one times. Although the words have a cognitive aspect, more than intellectual assent is involved. Commitment or trust is also included. (See 10:10 for the verb and 4:5 for the noun.)

Foreknow. Of five occurrences in the New Testament, two are in Romans (8:29 and 11:2). God is perfect in His intellectual life.

Foreordain. This means "to appoint beforehand." Of six occurrences in the New Testament, two are in Romans (8:29-30). (See note on "foreknow.")

Glorified. Its meaning is "to render glorious" or "to be full of honor." The verb occurs five times, the noun "glory" sixteen times. Mankind is guilty because men fail to give God the glory that is His due (1:21).

Gospel. The word occurs nine times in Romans, and the verb from which we get the noun occurs three times. Very literally, the verb means "to announce good things." Consequently, the noun indicates the content of that announcement—the "good news" or the "glad tidings." The book begins with a reference to the "gospel of God" and concludes (16:25) with a reference to "my gospel." Romans 1:16 is a classic statement about the gospel.

Grace. This occurs twenty-four times in Romans (the verb occurring once, 8:32). Grace is "unmerited favor" or "everything for nothing for those who deserve the exact opposite." Romans 3:24 assures us that the believer is justified freely by grace.

Heaven. It occurs just twice (1:18 and 10:6), and means "the abode of God."

Heirs. Such is "one who receives a portion of a position" (8:17).

Hope. In the New Testament, "hope" is far more than wish or desire. It is "confident expectation." Romans 5:2 says, "we . . . rejoice in hope (confident expectation) of the glory of God" (KJV). The word is used eleven times in this epistle.

Intercession. This interesting word is used only five times in the New Testament, and three of the five are in Romans. It means "to turn to"; "to approach"; "to come between"; and "to petition." Hence, in relation to God it means "to pray" (8:27, 34; 11:2).

Judgment. The word may mean simple "decision" or it may mean a decision against one—hence, "condemnation." (See Rom. 2:2, where the word could be translated either way.) It is used six times in Romans.

Justify. The word means "to declare righteous." The noun "righteousness" comes from this verb. Occurring fifteen times in Romans, it is one of the key terms in the book. (See Rom. 4:5 for the noun and verb.)

Legal or *Semi-Legal Terms.* Paul's letter to the Romans is without doubt the most carefully crafted of his writings. Forensic in nature, it is characterized by careful argument. Little wonder, then, that it contains terms such as "without excuse," which is one word in the Greek text and occurs only two times in the New Testament (1:20 and 2:1). "Condemnation" occurs three times in Romans and nowhere else (5:16, 18; 8:1). Paul uses the verb "to condemn" five times and four of those are in Romans. All of the three occurrences of the verb variously translated "to confirm"; "testify with"; or "also bearing witness" are in Romans (2:15; 8:16; 9:1). Add to this the legal overtones of the cluster of words under "concepts," and the fact that the word "law" occurs seventy-one times. As a result, the forensic character of the book becomes readily apparent.

Lord. This occurs no less than forty-four times. It signifies One with ultimate authority. The cognate verb occurs only seven times in the New Testament and four of those are in Romans. In 6:9, death *rules;* in 6:14, sin *rules;* in 7:1, law *rules;* and in 14:9, Christ *rules* the living and the dead.

Mortal. Paul is the only New Testament writer to use this word. Two of its six occurrences are in Romans (6:12 and 8:11). The word comes from the verb "to die" and means "dying."

Peace. The word suggests quietness, unity, concord, two parties coming together without friction. Paul uses the word eleven times in this epistle, usually of the peace the believer has with God through Christ (5:1).

Prophet. "One who speaks on behalf of God." It is used three times in Romans and exclusively of the Old Testament prophets.

Propitiation. This is a rare but exceedingly important word. It is used only once in Romans (3:25) where it is translated "sacrifice of atonement." The word suggests both a satisfying of God's righteous requirement (propitiation) and a provision for man's sin (expiation).

Reckon or *Impute.* The KJV uses these two words to translate one of the most important words in this epistle. The word behind our English translations occurs thirty-nine times in the New Testament. It is used thirty-three times by Paul, and nineteen of those are in Romans. It means "to put to one's account." The NIV* uses six different terms to translate this rich word: "pass judgment," "regard," "credit to," "count," "consider," and "maintain."

Reconciliation. Of the New Testament writers, only Paul uses this word, and two of its four occurrences are in Romans (5:11 and 11:15). Similarly, the verb "to reconcile" is used only by Paul and two of the six times it is used are in Romans (both times in 5:10). The word means to change from enmity to friendship or effect reparation for injury done.

Redemption. This significant theological term occurs twice (3:24 and 8:23). The word suggests release by ransom.

Repentance. Surprisingly enough, the word occurs only once (2:4), and the verb "to repent" not at all. The word means "a change of mind" in relation to God's truth and one's conduct.

Resurrection. The word occurs only two times in Romans (1:4 and 6:5). But note other terminology such as "God raised him from the dead." The word means a "standing or rising up."

Righteousness, Justify, Justification. All of these words are derived from the same stem. This is perhaps the most significant family of words in the entire epistle. The noun "righteousness" occurs

New International Version.

thirty-four times, eight of which are in the phrase "the righteous-ness of God." The verb "to justify" occurs fifteen times. There are two separate and distinct words from this stem, which are trans-lated "justification" in our English renditions. The more familiar one is used ten times in the New Testament and five times in Romans. The other is used two times in Romans and nowhere else in the Bible. To be "justified" is to have the righteousness of God reckoned to one's account. That is the key concept in the book of Romans, especially chapters 4 and 5.

Saints. This is an interesting word in that it serves as a noun, "saint," or as an adjective, "holy." The word occurs twenty-one times.

Salvation. The noun occurs five times and the verb "to save" eight times. In every case the reference is to the salvation of the soul. In the well-known verses, Romans 10:9-10, we find the verb in verse 9 and the noun in verse 10.

Sanctify. This important word means "to set apart" or "to make holy" and occurs just once (15:16).

Sin. Of nine words for sin in the New Testament, seven are used by Paul in Romans. This in itself shows how important the concept is to the argument of the book. In all, words which might be trans-lated "sin" occur a total of sixty-three times. The precise meanings of the individual words include "missing the mark," "transgress-ing," "lawlessness," "offense," and "disobedience." Taken together, these distinctions provide an adequate definition of sin.

Spirit. This word is found thirty-two times in this epistle and is used of the human spirit (1:9) as well as of the Holy Spirit (5:5).

Spiritual Gifts. It is important to note that this word comes from the same stem as the word "grace." The spiritual gifts are those gifts which God by His Spirit bestows. Hence, eternal life is a spiritual gift (6:23). Romans 12:6 refers to the variety of gifts. The word occurs six times.

Truth. The word occurs eight times, three of which are in the phrase "the truth of God."

Unrighteousness. The word occurs seven times in Romans, twice in 1:18. The word means "the lack of right conduct" or "wickedness."

NOTE

1. William Barclay, *The Letter to the Romans* (Philadelphia: Westminster, 1975), p. 7.

From the death of Paul to this day there has not been a Sabbath when he was not read, recited or quoted in the public ministrations of God's house; and so it will be to the end of time. Devils and wicked men, as well as saints and angels still say, "Jesus I know and Paul I know." The power of Jesus as a teacher arose from the fact that he was the author of truth, and the embodiment of truth, and knew what was in man, and spoke as man never spoke. The secret of Paul's power as a teacher is found, not merely or chiefly in his genius, though that was prodigious, nor in his acquaintance with Hebrew and Grecian lore, though that was vast, but in his thorough instruction by the abundance of visions and revelations, which he had from the Lord Jesus and from the large measure of God's Spirit granted him during his whole Christian life. Thus he was able with great clearness, directness, pungency and tenderness to address men orally and by writing.[1]

William S. Plumer

7

Special Study Projects

In this epistle there are no less than 219 words that do not occur in any other of Paul's letters; and of those, 94 do not occur anywhere else in the New Testament. The following 94 words are listed alphabetically, according to their spelling in the Greek text:

"wild olive tree" (11:17-24)

"inexpressible" (8:26)

"impenitent" (2:5)

"proportion" (12:6)

"without excuse" (2:1; 1:20)

"unmerciful" (1:31)

"unsearchable" (11:33)

"coals" (12:20)

"without law" (2:12)

"forbearance" (2:4)

"warring against" (7:23)

"abhorring" (12:9)

"severity" (11:22)

"cursing" (3:14)

"infirmities" (15:1)

"asps" (3:13)

"perfidious" (1:31)

"come abroad" (16:19)

"become unprofitable" (3:12)

"righteous judgment" (2:5)

"used deceit" (3:13)

"in bondage" (6:19)

"a hundred years" (4:19)

"burned" (1:27)

"were broken out" (11:17, 19-20)

"stretched out" (10:21)

"grafted in" (11:17, 19, 23-24)

"reminding" (15:15)

"are covered" (4:7)

"a longing" (15:23)

"art named" (2:17)

"inventors" (1:30)

"whether" (6:16)

"divinity" (1:20)

"hateful to God" (1:30)

"a trap" (11:9)

"delight" (7:22)

"bearing witness with" (2:15; 8:16, 9:1)

"groans together" (8:22)

"ruin" (3:16)

"travails together" (8:22)

"more boldly" (15:15)

"makes intercession" (8:26)

"to be high minded" (12:3)

"remnant" (9:27)

"kindly affectioned" (12:10)

"kind speaking" (16:18)

"whisperers" (1:29)
"commit sacrilege" (2:22)
"administering in sacred
   service" (15:16)
"cheerfulness' (12:8)
"are perceived" (1:20)
"newness" (6:4; 7:6)
"evil dispositions" (1:29)
"a good olive tree" (11:24)
"condemnation"
   (5:16, 18; 8:1)
"slanderers" (1:30)
"slumber" (11:8)
"dug down" (11:3)
"throat" (3:13)
"remnant" (11:5)
"became vain" (1:21)
"changed" (1:25-26)
"lawgiving" (9:4)
"lust" (1:27)
"oldness" (7:6)
"is present with" (7:18, 21)
"passing by" (3:25)
"thing formed" (9:20)
"that had before taken
   place" (3:25)
"first gave" (11:35)
"are we better?" (3:9)

"going before" (12:10)
"forefather" (4:1)
"reception" (11:15)
"succorer" (16:2)
"prophetic" (16:26)
"reverenced" (1:25)
"hardens" (2:5)
"counsellor" (11:34)
"conjoined" (6:5)
"strive together with"
   (15:30)
"may be refreshed with"
   (15:32)
"may be glorified together"
   (8:17)
"bow down" (11:10)
"to be comforted together"
   (1:12)
"cutting short" (9:28)
"consent" (7:16)
"slaughter" (8:36)
"married" (7:2)
"we more than overcome"
   (8:37)
"under judgment" (3:19)
"was left" (11:3)
"divine answer" (11:4)
"lie" (3:7).[2]

THE VALUE AND METHOD OF MAKING BIBLE CHARTS

A chart of biblical content can be likened to a mariner's map. It is an aid in navigating the ocean of biblical content. Such a method is not intended to eliminate outlining, paraphrasing, or memorizing, but rather is designed to supplement other methods. It is one of many ways of summarizing and preserving one's thoughts and feelings.

Charts take advantage of visual appeal, thereby utilizing another channel of learning. They provide a basis for teaching large units of material in a limited amount of time. There are many advantages to using charts while studying and presenting Bible material. Since they appeal to the eye, they are more readily remembered than words. Charts provide a helpful perspective since they enable one to see the whole as a sum of the parts.

A chart provides opportunity for emphasizing contrasts, repetition and position. For the viewer, it is especially advantageous in that ideas can be grasped at a glance. The viewer is delivered from the side roads of detail and directed along a highway of the dominant points of emphasis.

When making Bible charts, it is important to keep the charts inductive. That will assure that the structure of the biblical material determines the structure of the chart. A good chart should reveal not only the structural relations within biblical units, but also the effects of contextual material such as items of geography.

The individual making the chart should include only major terms, relations, and ideas. Beware of including so many details that the main emphasis is clouded.

Charts should be synthetical in nature and purpose. By that we mean that they should not merely indicate the parts, but should unify parts into one presentation. They should be readable from a common vantage point. References should be noted on the chart. The chart should be self-explanatory. They should be constructed in proportion to the amount of biblical material they represent. In general, a chart should be simple, clear, and intelligible. It should reveal the dominant aims and ideas. It should synthesize as well as analyze.

Many types of material can be placed on charts with profit to the student. Some of those might include: the main divisions of a book, subject, or period of history; a dominant theme and how the parts contribute to that theme; pivotal events and key chapters and verses; chapter and paragraph titles; relationships between various Bible books; the main lessons or possible applications of a portion of Scripture.

Notes

1. William S. Plumer, *Commentary on Romans* (Grand Rapids: Kregel, 1971), Introduction.
2. W. G. Scroggie, *Know Your Bible* (London: Pickering & Inglis, 1950), pp. 172-73.

Part III

Using a "Stethoscope" to Search for Heartwarming Ideas in the Epistle

No portion of the sacred writing is more appropriate for our times than Paul's Epistle to the Romans. Through its prayerful study sinners will be justified by faith, and Christians will be established in the fundamental doctrines of the grace of God.[1]

Louis T. Talbot

8

Constructing a Message

We have now surveyed the landscape of the epistle to the Romans by means of the "telescope" and have focused the "microscope" on a number of intriguing specifics and details of the epistle. The third section of the book will encourage us to use the "stethoscope" to find for ourselves heartwarming truths upon which to feed and organize material in the epistle in order to facilitate teaching and proclamation.

When constructing a devotional message it is wise to formulate what speakers refer to as a proposition or thesis. That will be a simple sentence that summarizes the content and impact of the message.

The proposition will be developed into a message by use of one of four interrogative words: why, how, when, or where. Study the passage that forms the basis for the message to discover which of those four words best characterizes the content.

The main points of the message are characterized by a key word, a noun in plural form that answers the interrogative and also characterizes the points of the message. Each main point should be undergirded by chapter and verse from the Bible passage. Since the main points should be timeless in nature, no names other than deity should be included. Each main point should be applied to the listener before going to the next point.

The conclusion of the message should provide the listener with a summary and a clear objective for the presentation of the message. The conclusion will combine the proposition with purpose.

The last part of the message to be written is the introduction. Until you have outlined the message, there is nothing to introduce. Begin the message where the people live. You should begin a message with the secular and conclude with the spiritual application.

What follows are outlines and reflections from Romans that the preacher could develop into finished sermons by carefully following the above procedure.

The interested reader should note Dr. Lloyd Perry's *Biblical Preaching for Today's World* (particularly chapters 1-3).[2]

SEED THOUGHTS

By These Be Known (1:1-17)
    Paul's credentials   (1:1-7)
    Paul's concern   (1:8-15)
    Paul's confidence   (1:16-17)
Good News of Grace (1:1, 9, 16)
    The gospel of God   (1:1)
    The gospel of His Son   (1:9)
    The gospel of Christ   (1:16)
These Are Important (1:1-2, 7)
    God   (1:1)
    Son   (1:2)
    Saint   (1:7)
Paul's Attitude Toward Other Believers (1:8-12)
Essential Elements of the Christian Life (1:8-15)
    Thanksgiving   (1:8)
    Interest   (1:8)
    Sincerity   (1:9)
    Prayer   (1:9-10)
    Fellowship   (1:11-12)
    Eagerness   (1:13)
    Indebtedness   (1:14)
    Readiness   (1:15)
Paul's Yearning (1:11-14)
    Its object   (1:11)
    Its obstacles   (1:13)
    Its obligation   (1:14)
The Righteousness of God (1:17— 16:27)
    Needed by sinful men   (1:17—3:20)
    Provided by God   (3:21-26)
    Received through faith   (3:27—4:25)
    Experienced in the soul   (5:1—8:17)
    Guaranteed as a permanent blessing   (8:18-39)
    Rejected by the Jewish nation   (9-11)
    Manifested in practical living   (12-16)
Pride in an Age of Power (1:16)
The World of Paganism (1:18-28)
Without Excuse (1:18-20)
An Interesting Paradox (1:20)

Wise Fools (1:22)
Turning Away from God (1:21-32)
Characteristics of the Natural World (1:21-22, 28; 8:6-7; 12:3)
  Darkness   (1:21)
  Distorted worship   (1:22)
  A reprobate mind   (1:28)
  Characterized by death   (8:6)
  War with God   (8:6-7)
  A carnal mind   (8:7)
  A conceited mind   (12:3)
The Old Heart (1:18-32); *(The New Heart* — 1 John 4:7-21)
They Changed the Glory of God into Idolatry (1:19-23; result v. 24)
They Changed the Truth of God into a Lie (1:25; result vv. 26-27)
They Gave Up the Knowledge of God (1:28; result vv. 29-32)
Where Shall Righteousness Be Found? (1:19—3:20)
  Not in natural religion (1:19—2:16)
    Corrupted by idolatry   (1:21-32)
    Permeated by hypocrisy   (2:1-16)
  Not in revealed religion (2:17—3:20)
    Jews did not keep the law   (2:17-29)
    Jews guilty under the law   (3:1-20)
All Stand Condemned (1:18—3:8)
  The heathen   (1:18-32)
  The good people   (2:1-16)
  The religious people   (2:17—3:8)
Condemnation (1:18-32) *(They knew God* — 1:18-20)
  They glorified Him not as God   (1:21-23)
  They changed the truth of God   (1:24-25)
  They rejected the knowledge of God   (1:26-32)
The Great Court Trial (1:16—3:20)
  The complaint   (1:18-32)
  The case   (2:1—3:8)
    The Gentile   (2:1-16)
    The Jew   (2:17—3:8)
  The verdict   (3:9-20)
  The only plea   (1:16-17)
Critics Will Be Condemned (2:1-11)
The World of Moralism (2:1-11)
The Moralist (2:1-16)
Principles of Judgment (2:1-16)
  The certainty of judgment
  The universality of judgment

The principles of judgment
The results of judgment
God's Principles of Judgment (2:1-29)
　According to God's truth, not man's opinion　　　　　(2:1-5)
　According to a man's deeds, not his status　　　　　(2:6-15)
　According to the gospel of Christ, not man's religion　(2:16-29)
Conscience Will Be the Judge (2:12-16)
Privilege Brings Responsibility (2:17-29)
The World of Judaism (2:17-21)
Outward Profession Will Not Help (2:17-24)
Only Genuine Obedience Counts (2:25-29)
The Righteousness of God (3:22, 24, 30; 4:1—5:21)
　The channel: Christ　　　　　　　　　　　　　　(3:22)
　The source: grace　　　　　　　　　　　　　　　(3:24)
　The application: faith　　　　　　　　　　　　　(3:30)
　The illustration: Abraham　　　　　　　　　　　(4:1-25)
　The results: blessings　　　　　　　　　　　　　(5:1-21)
The Advantage of Religious Training (3:1-19)
Objections Met (3:1-8)
　First objection　　　　　　　　　　(3:1) (Answer, 3:2)
　Second objection　　　　　　　　　(3:3) (Answer, 3:4)
　Third objection　　　　　　　　　　(3:5) (Answer, 3:6)
Right in God's Sight (3:21—5:21)
　The medium of righteousness　　　　　　　　　　(3:21-3:31)
　The basis of righteousness　　　　　　　　　　　(4:1-25)
　The attainment of righteousness　　　　　　　　(5:1-21)
Bad News: Condemnation Under Sin (3:1-20)
Good News: Justification by Faith (3:21-31)
　Apart from the law　　　　　　　　　　　　　　(3:21)
　Available through Christ　　　　　　　　　　　　(3:22-26)
　Accepted by faith　　　　　　　　　　　　　　　(3:27-31)
The World of Humanism—All Mankind Found Guilty (3:9-20)
Righteousness Revealed—God's Provision (3:21-31)
Justification: Three Essential Elements (3:24-25, 28)
　Justified by grace—Father provides it　　　　　　(3:24)
　Justified by blood—Son procures it　　　　　　　(3:25)
　Justified by faith—Spirit appropriates it　　　　　(3:28)
Righteousness by Faith (3:20-26)
The Blessedness of Sins Forgiven (4:1-8)
Justified (4:1-25)
　By faith, not by works of morality　　　　　　　(4:1-8)
　By faith, not by ordinances　　　　　　　　　　(4:9-12)

By faith, not by obedience to the law (4:13-25)
An Old Testament Precedent (4.1-25)
Appropriation of Righteousness (4:1-25)
  By faith, not by works of morality (4:1-8)
  By faith, not by rites of religion (4:9-12)
  By faith, not by deeds of the law (4:13-23)
  By faith in the death and resurrection of Christ (4:24-25)
The Promise Is to All (4:9-16)
Justification (4:1-25)
  How (4:1-8)
  Who (4:9-17)
  When (4:18-25)
Contrasts (4:1-25)
  Faith and works (4:1-8)
  Law and grace (4:9-17)
  Life and death (4:18-25)
Precious Possessions (5:1-2)
  Peace for the past
  Grace for the present
  Glory for the future
Products of Justification (5:1-11)
  Peace (5:1)
  Access to God (5:2)
  Rejoicing (5:2)
  Glory (5:3)
  Love of God (5:5)
  Saved from wrath (5:9)
  Joy in God (5:11)
Justification (5:1-21)
  The blessings of justification (5:1-11)
  The basis of justification (5:12-21)
The Love of God (5:3-8)
Saved from Wrath (5:9-11)
Grace is Free (5:12-18)
The Reign of Righteousness (5:12-21)
Grace is Abundant (5:19-21)
Questions and Answers (6:1-23)
  Rhetorical question (6:1) (Answer, 6:2-4)
  Rhetorical question (6:15) (Answer, 6:16-23)
The Way of Holiness (6:1 — 8:39)
The Victorious Life in Christ (6:1 — 8:39)
  In principle (6:1 — 7:6)

In practice (7:7-25)
In power (8:1-39)
A New Life in Christ (6:1-11)
Union with Christ in the Body (6:1-14)
Know—information (6:3-10)
Reckon—calculation (to take account) (6:11-12)
Yield—regimentation (arrange for service) (6:13-14)
Identification with Christ (6:3-5; 8:30)
In death (6:3)
In burial (6:4)
In resurrection (6:4-5)
In glorification (8:30)
The Meaning of Baptism (6:3-14)
Dead But Alive (6:8-11)
Yielding to God (6:12-16)
A New Loyalty to Christ (6:12-23)
Our Union with Christ (6:15-23)
New problem (6:15)
New obligations (6:16-18)
New duties (6:19-20)
New rewards (6:21-23)
The Gift of God (6:22-23)
Limitations of the Law (7:1-25)
Two husbands (7:1-6)
Two discoveries (7:7-14)
Two principles (7:15-25)
Freedom from Law (7:1-25)
A Life of Defeat (7:7-25)
The Death Struggle of Self (7:7-25)
The Conflict Within (7:14-25)
Three Confessions (7:14-25)
Statement, proof and conclusion (7:14-17)
Statement, proof and conclusion (7:18-20)
Statement, proof and conclusion (7:21-25)
Blessed Assurances (8:1-34)
A new position—"in Christ" (8:1-4)
A new power—"Holy Spirit" (8:5-25)
A new privilege—"prayer" (8:26-34)
Life in the Spirit (8:1-17)
The Holy Spirit Gives (8:1-30)
Victory over sin and death (8:1-11)
Witness to adoption (8:12-17)

Completion of salvation   (8:18-25)
Successful intercession   (8:26-30)
More Than Conquerors (8:1-39)
  No condemnation   (8:1-4)
  No obligation   (8:5-17)
  No separation   (8:18-39)
Sanctification (8:1-39)
  The power of sanctification   (8:1-17)
  The products of sanctification   (8:18-27)
  The praise of sanctification   (8:28-39)
The Carnal Mind (8:3-8)
Victory through the Spirit (8:5-25)
  The Spirit takes over our conflict with sin   (8:5-13)
  The Spirit secures our present position as sons   (8:14-17)
  The Spirit assures us the future glory as sons   (8:18-25)
Children of God (8:15-18)
The Glory to Come (8:18-30)
Guarantees of Glory (8:26-30)
Saved in His Love (8:29-39)
Righteousness Reviewed (8:31-39)
The Triumph of Faith (8:31-39)
Great Assurances (8:31-39)
  Their relation to God   (8:31b-33)
  Their relation to Christ   (8:34)
  Their relation to circumstances   (8:35-39)
Three Doxologies
  (8:38-39)
  (11:33-36)
  (16:26-27)
The Most Important Election (9:1-13)
  The blessings of election   (9:1-5)
  The basis of election   (9:6-13)
God's Purpose for His people (9:1-33)
  Paul's passion   (9:1-3)
  Israel's privilege   (9:4-5)
  God's purpose   (9:6-24)
  Gentile's position   (9:25-33)
Three Tenses for God's People (9:1—11:36)
  Election—past   (9:1-33)
  Rejection—present   (10:1-21)
  Restoration—future   (11:1-36)

Election (9:6-29)
  The principle of election   (9:6-13)
  The freedom of election   (9:14-21)
  The God of election   (9:22-29)
The Purpose of God (9:9-18)
Mercy and Judgment (9:14-18)
God's Rights in God's World (9:19-29)
The Sovereignty of God (9:19-25)
The Testimony of the Prophets (9:25-29)
The Children of the Living God (9:26-33)
The Mistake of the Jews (10:1-4)
Israel's Rejection (10:1-21)
  The reason   (10:1-13)
  The remedy   (10:14-17)
  The result   (10:18-21)
Israel, Its Present (10:1-21)
  The ignorance of the way of salvation   (10:1-11)
  The ignorance of the application of salvation (10:12-13)
  The ignorance of the proclamation of salvation (10:14-21)
The Righteousness of God (10:3-13)
The Word of Faith (10:5-10)
The Universal Promise (10:11-13)
The Nature of Faith (10:14-21)
Proofs of a Future for Israel (11:1-36)
  The personal proof   (11:1)
  The historical proof   (11:2-10)
  The dispensational proof   (11:11-24)
  The scriptural proof   (11:25-36)
The Wisdom of God (11:26-36)
A Doxology to Theology (11:33-36)
A Hymn of Praise to God (11:33-36)
  Praise of God's knowledge   (11:33*b*)
  Praise of God's wisdom   (11:34)
  Praise of God's riches   (11:35-36)
The Character of Consecration (12:1)
  Voluntary—"present"
  Complete—"your bodies"
  Sacrifical—"a sacrifice"
  Practical—"your service"
  Rational—"your reasonable service"
The Christian and the World (12:1-21)

Evidences of a Christian Life (12:1 — 13:7)
   Complete consecration   (12:1-2)
   Wise use of gifts   (12:3-8)
   Perfect love   (12:9-21)
   Subjection to civil power   (13:1-7)

The Practice of Righteousness (12:1 — 15:13)
   In Christian duties   (12:1-21)
   In civil duties   (13:1-7)
   In social duties   (13:8-14)
   In fraternal duties   (14:1 — 15:13)

Duties of the Justified (12:1-21)
   To God   (12:1-2)
   To ourselves   (12:3)
   To the church   (12:4-8)
   To other Christians   (12:9-13)
   To the enemy   (12:14-21)

The Meaning of Christian Consecration (12:3-21)
   Humility in service   (12:3-8)
   Love for the brethren   (12:9-13)
   Love for the outsider   (12:14-21)

Duties to God and Fellow Believers (12:3-21)
   Think soberly
   Minister diligently
   Love sincerely

The Stewardship of Service (12:6-8)

Be Aglow with the Spirit (12:11)

Harmony But Not Uniformity (12:16)

Coping in Today's World (12:16-20)

The Christian and the State — Christian Citizenship (13:1-7)

God's Alarm Clock (13:12)

Duties of Christian Citizens (13:1-10)
   Loyalty   (13:1-7)
   Love   (13:8-10)

Civil Duties (13:1-14)
   Obedience   (13:1-7)
   Love   (13:8-10)
   The motivation which produces obedience and love   (13:11-14)

Duties of the Justified (13:1-14)
   To the state   (13:1-7)
   To the neighbors   (13:8-14)

The Christian Life in Days of Crisis (13:11-14)

The Christian and Questionable Things (14:1—15:7)
    Am I fully convinced?   (14:1-5)
    Am I doing this unto the Lord?   (14:6-9)
    Will it stand the test at the judgment seat?   (14:10-12)
    Am I causing others to stumble?   (14:13-21)
    Am I doing this by faith?   (14:22-23)
    Am I pleasing myself or others?   (15:1-7)
Freedom of Conscience (14:1-6)
Liberty in the Christian Life (14:1-13a)
Christian Service vs. Doubtful Questions (14:3-23)
    The principle of personal liberty   (14:3-13a)
    The principle of our neighbor's good   (14:13b-21)
    The principle of God's glory   (14:22-23)
Individual Responsibility (14:5-12)
The Philosophy of Toleration (14:13-23)
Seeking Peace (14:16-19)
Responsible Faith (14:20-23)
Pleasing Others (15:1-3)
Accept One Another (15:1-13)
    The imitation of Christ   (15:1-7)
    Christian brotherhood   (15:8-13)
Glorifying God (15:4-13)
The Romance of the Ministry (15:14-19)
The Christian as a Worker (15:14-33)
    A worker's motives   (15:14-16)
    A worker's vindication   (15:17-21)
    A worker's plans   (15:22-29)
    A worker's need   (15:30-33)
Marks of Ministry (15:14-33)
    Personal   (15:14-17)
    Powerful   (15:18-21)
    Purposeful   (15:22-29)
    Prayerful   (15:30-33)
A Worker (15:22-29)
    His difficulties
    His desire
    His delight
    His duty
    His dependence
A Servant of the Church (16:1-2)
A Galaxy of Saints (16:3-16)

Take Note of These People (16:1-24)
   Some friends to greet (16:1-16)
   Some foes to avoid (16:17-20)
   Some faithful to honor (16:21-24)
Parting Words (16:17-20)
   A word of warning (16:17-18)
   A word of praise (16:19)
   A word of promise (16:20*a*)
The Outward Look (16:17-24)
A Salute to the Saints (16:21-24)
Glory Belongs to God (16:21-27)
The Upward Look—A Doxology (16:25-27)
The Mystery of God (16:25-27)

NOTES

1. Louis T. Talbot, *Address on Romans* (Wheaton, Ill.: Van Kampen, 1936), Foreword.
2. Lloyd M. Perry, *Biblical Preaching for Today's World* (Chicago: Moody, 1973).

When I first became pastor of the Philadelphia church I began my ministry by preaching on the Epistle to the Romans. For three and one-half years I never took a text outside of the Epistle to the Romans. I saw the church transformed; the audience filled the pews and then the galleries; and the work went on with great blessing. But just as important as the transformation of the church there was the transformation of the preacher.[1]

Donald Grey Barnhouse

9

Devotional Ideas

The meditations that follow are reflections by the authors on various themes and patterns within the epistle to the Romans. Some are more fully developed than others, but each is designed to be illustrative of the riches the epistle yields rather than definitive expositions or finely polished homilies. If the reader finds his heart stirred with fresh truth and his mind quickened to pursue further a line of thought, the aim of this segment will have been accomplished.

HOW'S YOUR APPETITE?
Introducing the book of Romans
(Romans 1:1-7)

Picture yourself at a restaurant in Japan getting ready to order dinner. Familiar with neither Japanese food nor the language, you wonder how you are going to know what to order when out of the corner of your eye you see the restaurant's window display. To your great delight you discover that before your eyes, in living color and actual size, are numbered wax replicas of all the items on the menu. Now you know what you are going to eat, and your appetite is ready!

The apostle Paul had never been to Rome, so when he wrote this epistle to say some very important things, he first gave them an "appetizer" to establish his credibility. He *introduced himself* by name; he gave his credentials as one of them—a slave of Jesus Christ (a hint that in this epistle he will contrast the slave of Christ and the slave of sin); but he also made it clear that he was not just anybody—he was an apostle with authority behind what he said.

Next, he got right to the "meat and potatoes." He *introduced the gospel*. Its source is found in God's promises long ago through His prophets in the Old Testament Scriptures (a hint that throughout the letter he will remind them of this, usually by "it is written," which occurs no less than fifteen times!).

Paul pointed out that the substance of the gospel concerns the person of Jesus Christ—a Jew, a human being born of Mary, but the

151

divine Son of God born of the Holy Spirit. His proof? That Jesus Christ is God has authentication in His resurrection from the dead—a historical fact!

Then he offered some "side dishes" in the benefits of grace, which come only because of Jesus Christ and through Jesus Christ. But with those goes the responsibility of mission in spreading the good news of the gospel to the Gentiles (a hint that he will deal with Jew and Gentile as in none of his other writings).

A "salad" perked up the appetite when Paul said that the results of this gospel would be to lead them to faith and obedience to Jesus Christ (a hint that he will deal with the practical outworking of personal faith in the last third of the book).

As the first layer of "dessert" he *introduced the recipients* of the epistle, and he gave them the encouragement that they were not alone—they were part of a world wide fellowship of believers. The next layer pointedly reminded them that he was writing to believers in Rome (a hint that in the last chapter he will enunciate many of them by name with intriguing clues about race, occupation, and social standing). The rich "filling" came when he said that they were not just called to be saints—to live holy, saintly lives—but they were, in fact, saints because they were partakers of Christ's righteousness (a hint that justification will be a major theme in his epistle)!

Paul knew how to top it off with a dollop of rich "cream" as he pronounced grace and peace from God to be theirs as beneficiaries of God's favor.

By now we should understand that Paul was not just writing to the saints in Rome. He was writing with *you* in mind. The Spirit of God would have you read it, study it, digest it, and grow by it.

Has Paul's "menu for a fabulous feast" stirred your appetite to dig in and feed on the riches of the book of Romans?

HOW RIGHTEOUS CAN YOU GET?
(Romans 3:21-26)

Language is an interesting thing. Words listed as synonyms in the dictionary can take on decidedly different meanings, depending on the context. For instance, one is flattered to be called "levelheaded," whereas he feels otherwise about being called "flatheaded." A girl may blush when a young man tells her, "Time stops when I look at you," but she may do something else if he says, "Your face would stop a clock!"

Two key words in Romans need careful watching—*law* and *righteousness*. "Law" occurs twice in one verse but with different meanings. The "righteousness of God" occurs four times and is without doubt the key phrase, but it is used in two decidedly different ways. Verses 21 through 26 are in the Greek text all one grammatically complicated sentence, the heart of which is, "But now . . . the righteousness of God has been manifested . . . for the demonstration . . . of His righteousness at the present time." That kind of righteousness, then, was not the intrinsic righteousness of God's character revealed in the Old Testament, but God's righteousness disclosed *at the present time*—Paul's time.

What, we ask, has revealed this unique righteousness now? Paul answers that it is *in the gospel* (Rom. 1:17) that it is made known. The good news of the gospel does not tell us that God is a righteous God. That has already been revealed, and for sinful man that is not good news. What the gospel does make known is something quite different. It is wonderful and astounding news.

Paul defines righteousness from God first *negatively* when he tells us what it is not, and then *positively* when he tells us what it is. It is not the righteousness of the law, or lawkeeping. In Philippians 3:6 Paul says that he was faultless in relation to that legalistic righteousness, and later in that chapter he says that he counts that righteousness of lawkeeping as garbage in relation to the surpassing greatness of the righteousness that comes from God by faith!

The righteousness of the law says, "Do" whereas the righteousness of Christ says, "Believe." The righteousness of the law says, "Work and become good" and the righteousness of Christ says, "Receive Christ and be reckoned good."

After Paul so clearly distinguishes between the righteousness of Christ and the righteousness of the law he seems to throw us a curve when he says that the righteousness of Christ is *witnessed to by the law and the prophets!* What we must see, of course, is *not* that principle of law or lawkeeping, but rather it is the books of the law in the Old Testament which are now in focus.

The law and the prophets in the Old Testament continually testify (present tense) to the righteousness of Christ. No doubt there are many figures and types to which we could point, but surely Paul has Abraham in mind. In the very next chapter he deals at length with his experience and strongly emphasizes that Abraham was justified well before the giving of the law.

Paul says that the prophets, too, testify to Christ's righteousness even as Peter said in Acts 10:43, "To him give all the prophets witness, that through his name whosoever believeth in him shall receive remission of sins" (KJV). In Romans 4, Paul uses David as an illustration from the books of the prophets as one who was a recipient of righteousness.

Now Paul tells us exactly what that righteousness is (Rom. 3:22). It is a righteousness *from God*. In verse 24 we learn that all who believe are "justified freely by his grace" (KJV). The truth so simply stated here is elaborated in chapter 4. God's righteousness is reckoned to our account or imputed to us. Even more clearly, in 1 Corinthians 1:30 he says that "Christ Jesus, . . . who became to us . . . righteousness" and in 2 Corinthians 5:21, God "made him [Jesus] who knew no sin to be sin on our behalf, that we might become the righteousness of God in Him."

So being made righteous ("justification") is more than becoming just as a "person who had never sinned" before God. That would leave me yet in my own righteousness which is as "filthy rags." Rather, it is standing before our holy God in the very righteousness of Jesus Christ himself!

The glorious part of this truth in our sentence is that since God has acted in our behalf, God's righteousness is freely dispensed. The word translated "freely" (KJV) here is the "without reason" of John 15:25. This righteousness becomes ours *through faith in Jesus Christ* (Rom. 3:22). It becomes ours not by working, but by believing; not by our trying, but by our receiving!

Romans 3:23 is one of the most familiar verses in the entire Bible. It assures us that righteousness is available to *everyone who believes* without distinction. The fact that we are sinners before God without any righteousness of our own is enough to make us candidates.

Grammatically speaking, the last phrase of verse 22 and all of verse 23 are parenthetical. Enclose them in parentheses and then go back and read the text, skipping over the parenthesis. How beautifully the message flows: "Righteousness of God [comes] through faith in Jesus Christ for all those who believe . . . being justified as a gift by His grace through the redemption which is in Christ Jesus." Now the words in the parenthesis become the counterpoint to set in bold relief the glorious truth of the believer's justification!

There is an interesting change in tense within the parenthesis. "All have sinned" (past tense—as a matter of established fact) and all "fall short" (present tense—continually and constantly) of the glory of God. As Paul will develop later in the book of Romans, in Adam all of mankind fell—an established fact. The effects of that Fall are so pervasive that we continue to fall short in "right living" every day of our lives—a present reality.

But what does God's *glory* mean? It could imply "praise" or "approval." Although there is nothing in us to merit God's approval, let alone His praise, the thrust of our text is to assure us that in Christ we stand accepted, approved, even praised, since the praise due His Son is in some mysterious and wonderful way shared by those to whom Christ's righteousness is imputed.

We cannot get more righteous than that, and praise God, we need not be!

DOES GOD EVER OVERLOOK SIN?
(Romans 3:21-26)

God in a wonderful way reckons to the believer's account His very own righteousness. Until we see that, we cannot appreciate the grandeur of the gospel. But in this very same text we see a paradox presented in verse 26, and we ask ourselves how it can be that the righteous God can justify the sinner. How can the same God who pronounces sentence also be the one who acquits? Can God really be both prosecutor and defender when it comes to dealing with sin?

The noun "righteous" and the cognate verb "make righteous" are without doubt the most important words in the sentence, the stem occurring no less than seven times. That our translators translate the noun at times "righteousness" and at other times "justice" suggests the richness and complexity of the term.

God is utterly righteous. Twice in this sentence (vv. 25-26) there is the affirmation that God demonstrated the utter righteousness of the justice of His character. Yet, for sinful man (v. 23) it is small comfort indeed for, a righteous God cannot tolerate sin and declares that the soul that sins must die. God must judge sin, and whatsoever a man sows he must reap! The more we think about it, the greater the paradox and the more marvelous it becomes that the righteous God justifies "the one who has faith in Jesus" (v. 26). In our world justice is an exceedingly rare commodity, even changing its face according to conditions such as race, finances, or prestige. But since God is utterly righteous, He can do no other than to act in accordance with His nature. God acts righteously. He demonstrates His righteousness.

God has done so in relation to "sin previously committed" (v. 25), or the "sins that are past" (KJV). Does Paul mean those sins that were committed prior to conversion to Christ? If so, that would solve the problem of the past, but it would leave the sinner on his own from that point on. What a sad state of affairs!

No, the "sins that are past" (v. 25, KJV) refer to those sins committed by men and women of faith in times before the sacrifice of Christ. God "passed over" those sins. How could He possibly do that? Did He just overlook all of the sin committed up until Christ died on the cross? Did God act out of character—in violation of His intrinsic righteousness? After all, the Scriptures say that the blood of bulls and goats could never accomplish the forgiveness of sins.

It is imperative that we see the twofold use of the phrase, "for the demonstration . . . of His righteousness." In verse 25 He did so with forbearance in regard to sins of prior time, whereas in verse 26 He did it in the present time (Paul's time) so that He could be utterly righteous in His character and yet justify any and all who would believe. God could act as He did in relation to past times only on the basis of what He would do in this present time!

God presented Christ as a "sacrifice of atonement" (v. 25, NIV), thereby demonstrating that all of those sins committed in the past were not simply passed over but were passed *into* forgiveness on the basis of what He would ultimately do in Christ to atone for those sins. In other words, the saints of prior times were saved "on credit" or in anticipation of that perfect sacrifice!

The phrase "sacrifice of atonement" (v. 25) translates a single word in the Greek text, and is the key to resolving the paradox. It is one of the most significant, yet one of the most controversial, words in the entire New Testament. It occurs only here and in Hebrews 9:5, "place of atonement" (NIV). (The verb from which it is derived occurs just twice in the New Testament—Luke 18:13 and Heb. 2:17.)

The debate on this word has raged as to whether it should mean "expiation" or "propitiation." Expiation emphasizes that the offering of Christ blots out the sinner's transgression. In propitiation the movement is not toward man and his sin as in expiation, but toward God and emphasizes that the sacrifice of Christ has effected a change in His attitude toward man—that the sacrifice of Christ has satisfied God's holiness.

Rather than choose one those meanings, we must see that the word involves both expiation and propitiation. Only as we fathom the richness of the word do we see that God indeed acts justly in bestowing His righteousness upon sinful men. The "redemption which is in Christ Jesus" (v. 24), and "in His blood" (v. 25) reinforce that our Lord's great redemptive act is in focus.

The marvel is that God's righteousness flows freely to the believer! Because the ransom has been paid and the atonement accomplished on the basis of His redemptive act, God is "the justifier of the one who has faith in Jesus" (v. 26). The participle here is in the present tense denoting that it is God's continual and ongoing activity—our Lord's present glorious occupation as He justifies all who believe.

God cannot, and God does not, overlook sin. But He does look over sin and write *forgiven* for all who have faith in Jesus!

SHALL WE SIN BIG TO BE FORGIVEN BIG?
(Romans 6:1, 15)

We see the wonder of God's righteousness imputed whereby the sinner is declared righteous and shares in the very righteousness of Jesus Christ. We see the splendor of that truth highlighted in the intrinsic righteousness of God's character and essence. In Romans 6 a question is posed. In fact, it is stated once in verse 1 and again in verse 15. What it boils down to is, If the more we sin, the more we are forgiven, should we sin big so that God can forgive big?

To this we say with Paul, "By no means! Absolutely unthinkable!" But under the pressure and tension of daily life, is the response always that clear? Is there temptation to rationalize away any offense by an assumption of "easy grace"?—in effect to say, "It's no big deal. God always forgives!"

What must be seen is that the result of God's righteousness imputed must be righteousness incarnate in the life of the believer. To answer Paul's question, the root must bear fruit. Since the root is justification, sanctification must follow. It is specifically stated, "But now having been freed from sin, . . . you derive your benefit, resulting in sanctification" (v. 22). The fruit is holiness. The implication is, if the root is there (justification), the fruit (holiness) will be there.

Having been *accounted* right the believer now moves on to *become* right. The change in tense of the verbs is most significant. You have been set free. This is a past act, a specific event, a once-and-for-all happening when as sinners we were pronounced righteous in Christ. But "you derive your benefit" is present tense and indicates a continuing and growing experience in the life of the believer. Justification is an act whereas sanctification is a process. The root is planted once, but fruit is to be borne continually. If the Holy Spirit indwells, then the fruit of the Spirit will be manifest.

The same truth is found in verse 16 as Paul states that obedience leads to righteousness. It leads not to imputed righteousness, but to personal righteousness, which is to be incarnated in the life of the believer.

To contemplate sinning in order that grace may abound is to fail to understand that we are rooted in Christ, both in His death and in His resurrection. "We . . . died to sin" (v. 2). The tense denotes a specific act in past time. The same statement is found in verse 7. But although the believer has died to sin, he is not *dead* to sin! Anyone who thinks he is dead to sin is in for a rude awakening.

When we read in the Bible that "our old self was crucified with him so that the body of sin might be rendered powerless" (v. 6, NIV), we need to ask when this happened. Verse 8 makes it plain that it is with Christ that we died.

How many were crucified at Calvary? Only Jesus and two thieves? Paul says that he, too, was crucified with Christ. He states that every believer was crucified there with Him. We were "baptized into His death" (v. 3). Though there are many different kinds of baptism in the Scriptures, the significance of baptism in every case is identification. Christ so completely identified with the sinner that in the mind of God the believer, too, was crucified. When Christ bore your sin, you were there! So to say, "Let's sin much in order to be forgiven much" is to insult God.

The believer is not only rooted in Christ's death, but also in His resurrection (vv. 4-5, 7-8).

Since we are rooted in Christ we are destined to bear fruit. The righteousness of Christ is to be incarnated in the daily walk of the believer. Our Lord's infinite resources are available to accomplish that. "Count yourselves dead to sin but alive to God in Christ Jesus" (v. 11, NIV). The verb "count" is the same word used in chapter 4 when Paul says that God "reckons" or imputes the righteousness of Christ to the believer's account. God has counted us righteous in Christ. Now we are to count ourselves righteous and demonstrate it by the way we live.

Unfortunately, the impact of the verb in verse 4 of the NIV doesn't come through clearly. "Just as Christ was raised from the dead through the glory of the Father, we too may live a new life." A more literal translation would be, "even so we should walk in newness of life." In the power of Christ's resurrection we are to begin walking in newness of life, and then to keep right on walking, continually and increasingly bearing the fruit of Christ's life rooted in us.

It is clear from this text that the way to conquer sin is not to struggle against it, engaging in a "daily dozen" to crucify the flesh. Rather, it is to cultivate and nurture the presence of Christ, allowing Him to bear His fruit in us and through us.

If the believer were, in fact, dead to sin there would be no need for the admonitions in verses 12 and 13. According to verse 7, when we died with Christ we were freed from the penalty of sin. But not until we die physically will we be freed from the allurement of sin. The present tense in the following verbs makes it clear that it is a matter of our daily walk and progress. *"Do not let sin reign* in your mortal body so that you obey its evil desires. *Do not offer* the parts of your body to sin, as instruments of wickedness, but rather offer yourselves to God . . . offer the parts of your body to him" (vv. 11-13, NIV). and allow this obedience to lead to righteousness (v. 16) as obedience always will.

MORE THAN CONQUERORS
(Romans 8:14-39)

Words of encouragement are needed more often than they are received. Why not adopt a slogan to which you can turn for encouragement whenever needed? The slogan that I would recommend is "Hypernikon."

My first contact with the word came when some fellow students in college tried to sell me a copy of the yearbook the name of which was the *Hypernikon.* After having shown my ignorance of Greek by confessing that I had never even heard of the word or knew of its meaning, I discovered it in the eighth chapter of Romans. From that day on I have found its truth a source of spiritual blessing.

Romans 8:37 reads "Nay, in all these things we are *more than conquerors* through him that loved us" (KJV). This blessed truth is hidden in one of the richest chapters of Scripture. The first four verses tell us that we have a new position in Christ. Verses 5 through 25 emphasize the new power we have through the Holy Spirit. The new privileges that are the possession of the Christian are listed in verses 26 through 39.

The sufferings of the present are not worth comparing with the glory that is to be revealed to us. The creation is waiting with eager longing for the revealing of the sons of God. The creation will then be set free from its bondage to decay and obtain the glorious liberty of the children of God. In this hope we were saved (Rom. 8:18-25). Great assurances encourage the child of God as he places his hope in Christ.

The child of God is sustained by God. In former times the Holy Spirit inspired men. "Men moved by the Holy Spirit spoke from God (2 Pet. 1:21, NIV). Now He is the daily consultant who intercedes for the believer. He helps us in our weakness (8:26a). When we do not know how to pray as we ought, He prays for us (8:26b). In both the infirmity of utterance and of ignorance, He intercedes for us. The Holy Spirit also intervenes on our behalf. Through the works of providence He makes all things work together for good to those who put their trust in Him (8:28). This verse unfolds the certainty, scope, continuity, unity, and result of God's gracious providence.

The child of God has been chosen by God (8:29-30). Five words appear in these two verses that are not included in the first seven chapters of Romans. They seem to form a chain from eternity to eternity. God foreknew in eternity and predestined or appointed us beforehand. He called us out of the world and justified us in the world. The fifth word states that God glorified us in the past tense. It is so certain that God had Paul inscribe it as though it was already an accomplished fact.

The child of God is kept by God. Four pointed questions appear in verses 31 through 35. Christ is the sufficient answer for each question. He is our protection (8:31-32), our perfection (8:33), our vindication (8:34), and our security (8:35). Tell me, shall tribulation, distress, persecution, famine, nakedness, peril, or sword ever be able to separate us from God? No, for in all these things we are more than conquerors. Hypernikon!

The Total Difference
(Romans 10:9-13)

Strange as it seems, many evangelicals loudly trumpet their commitment to an inerrant and verbally inspired Scripture, and yet remain uninterested in the fine points of the text that they affirm in its very word forms is inspired by God.

The significance of voice, tense, and mood in language usage is all but lost in our day.

Consider these first two verses, which are among the most familiar in the entire Bible. Many, if not most, Christians have committed them to memory. They contain nuances of grammar, which make a great difference and which may easily elude us and, as a result, distort meaning. "That if you *confess* with your mouth Jesus as Lord, and *believe* in your heart that God raised Him from the dead, you shall be saved; for with the heart man believes, resulting in righteousness, and with the mouth he confesses, resulting in salvation" (Rom. 10:9-10, italics added).

There is a significant difference in the *voice* of the verbs in these two verses that is not clear in the English translation. "Confess" and "believe" in verse 9 are repeated in verse 10. Whereas they are active voice in verse 9, they are passive in verse 10. What difference does that really make? It is the difference between "to kill" and "to be killed," "to praise" and "to be praised."

"If you confess" and "believe" (active voice) are activities in which you must participate if you are to reap the benefits. There must be commitment of will to do that. Individually and personally you must confess and believe in order to have salvation.

But verse 10 is in the passive voice: "With the mouth *it is confessed* and with the heart *it is believed*" (authors' translation). Here the focus is no longer on the individual who believes, but on the matter that is to be believed and confessed. *What you confess and believe makes a difference.*

What is the "it" of the text? Precisely what are we to confess and believe in order to gain salvation? To take God's Word seriously, we must put ourselves through the effort to find "it" in the context. We dare not suggest any good idea of our own but must get it from the text itself. Grammatically, we must find what it is that stands as the subject of the verb in verse 10. It is "the word of faith" back in verse 8. It is not confessing by mouth His name or saying that God is the source of all blessings—healing, a new job, a restored marriage, obedient children. "It" is the "word of faith," which Paul says he is preaching (v. 10).

What is that "word of faith"?

To understand "faith" in relation to "word," we may consider two grammatical options. One is to understand that Paul is referring to some matter of personal conviction that he is preaching. Certainly Paul would not preach anything about which he was not convinced.

The other, which is more likely, is to understand that Paul's message was far more than the proclamation of some subjective experience. Paul is affirming that the word that he preaches is a message he has objectively identified as to its content.

In the Greek text Paul employs a definite article with the word "faith." It is "the word of *the* faith." The "it" of our text is the objective statement of faith or doctrine, which is the heart of the Christian gospel! The apostle Jude speaks of "the faith which was once for all delivered to the saints (v. 3, NASB). It is that faith that must be confessed and believed if one is to enter the kingdom of God. Confessing and believing anything else will not do.

In Romans 10:11, the significance of *tense* must be noted to make clear its meaning. "He who believes in him will not be put to shame" (NIV). Literally, "the one who is believing" affirms that right now, at this moment, our trust and confidence must be in God, or we shall surely be ashamed and ultimately bring shame upon His name. *To be continually believing makes a difference.*

If someone says of a person suffering from malnutrition that he "eats rice," it does not necessarily mean that he *is* eating rice, nor even that he has rice to eat. He may be starving! Similarly, for the one who has been born again, that one act of having come to saving faith in Jesus Christ does not guarantee "no shame" if believing is not a fresh and present reality. It cannot be a matter of mere pointing to an act in the past. The tense emphasizes the urgency of faith's being moment-by-moment so that we will never be put to shame.

Actually, "never" may be a shade too strong. *"Will not be ashamed"* is a more accurate rendering. The strong contrast is between present believing and the possibility of future shame. Because this verb is future tense, it should be understood that the one who trusts *now* will not be ashamed *then*, in future time. Note that the verse begins, "For the Scripture says." What follows is a fragmentary quotation from Isaiah 28, where the scene is the judgment of almighty God. Although this chapter is not a simple text, and although it does blend history and prophecy, nevertheless the focus is judgment.

All of that reinforces the probability that what Paul has in mind here is that one who confesses and believes Christ in this life will not be ashamed on that day of divine judgment. "Whoever acknowledges me before men, I will also acknowledge him before my Father in heaven. But whoever disowns me before men, I will disown him before my Father in heaven," says the Lord (Matt. 10:32-33, NIV).

Yet, perhaps we should not throw out the word "never" too quickly. To allow it to stand does emphasize an important truth. As long as one is trusting he will never be ashamed. Conversely, the moment one ceases to trust he is a candidate for a shameful fall.

A third difference is found in a significant change in mood in Romans 10:13: "WHOEVER WILL CALL UPON THE NAME OF THE LORD WILL BE SAVED." "Whoever will call" (subjunctive) is a matter of calling or not calling. "Will be saved" (indicative) is a matter of certainty when the condition is met. We may or may not call on the Lord. We may choose to believe or we may choose to reject. We have that option. Some who hear the gospel will accept; others will not.

But how wonderful that (as in v. 9) there is a change in verse 11 from uncertainty to surety, leaving no room for doubt. The result is assured: If we believe, we *will be* saved. If we call upon the Lord *He will* respond. That is absolute and eternal. *The certainty of salvation makes a difference!*

After having considered the differences made clear by the grammar in these four verses, we see in verse 12 a matter where there is no difference! "For there is no distinction between Jew and Greek; for the same Lord is Lord of all, abounding in riches for all who call upon him." Here there is no difference! The gospel is for all, to be preached to all, and a gracious God will respond to all who call upon Him!

What difference does the truth in these verses make to you?

What God Wants of You
(Romans 12:1-2)

As many sermons may have been preached on this text as on any in all of Scripture. Because of its familiarity, it is easy for us to venerate it without examining it; to let it wash over us without listening to what it has to say.

We are confronted with an exceedingly strong appeal—the deep desire of the heart of God for the believer. To be sure, it is Paul's word, but the apostle is speaking for his God when he says, "I urge you." The verb he uses is the technical term used in ancient times to signal the main intent of a letter. "Beseech" or "beg" or "implore" would all be appropriate. Paul wants us to know that this is something that God deeply desires for the believer.

He makes his appeal on the basis of what God has done for us, that is, "by the mercies of God." It is God's "due." Paul takes us back to chapters 4 through 8, in which he carefully delineates the mercies of God. The word is plural, indicating that the more mercies received the more there are to receive.

The appeal is distinctly Christian. If you have tasted the mercies of God, it is to you. There is the astounding mercy of justification—God's declaring the sinner to be righteous in His sight (chap. 4); the peace and joy that flows from it (chap. 5); the new life the believer may enjoy in identification with his Lord (chap. 6); the strengthening of the Spirit and the victory over every foe that cause one to exult in Christ (chap. 8).

The rich content of these previous chapters is designed to prepare us to respond as the apostle tells us what it is that God desires of us. Paul proceeds to a *distinct directive* that is clear, specific, and pointed: "Offer your bodies as living sacrifices" (authors' translation). Our *bodies!* Now that is very intimate. We might have expected the apostle to say, "Offer your inner life, your heart, your soul, your will." But "bodies" is more ordinary and not quite what we would have had in mind. That word makes the appeal so very tangible, immediate, and personal! Does it seem strange that God wants your body? It suggests that the believer's body should be cared for more carefully, exercised more faithfully, and disciplined more consistently than many of us do.

But it is more likely that we should not understand the word "body" in too narrow a sense. Paul here, as occasionally elsewhere, seems to use the term not in contrast with the inner life, but rather as a term for the *totality* of life. Certainly Paul is not suggesting that God desires a literal slain sacrifice of actual flesh and bones.

There is, however, a strong connection between the body and the inner life. It is true enough that the body can be captive and the soul remain free, but it is certainly the case that when you give your body, your inner life is included. You may wonder what it really means to serve God with your body, but just try serving Him apart from your body! Furthermore, if you fully offer your body to God, will you not exercise prayerful judgment at those times when you may be tempted to go "in spirit" rather than make the effort to see that your body goes, too?

The offering that God desires is a living offering as opposed to slain or inanimate sacrifices. It is indeed a holy offering because the believer is reckoned to be holy by God and increasingly becomes holy in daily conduct through God's working within him. It is an offering "pleasing to God" because it is the total being, not just a piece of wealth or a possession.

It should be noted that the word is literally *"well*-pleasing," an offering that makes God happy, giving that pleases Him thoroughly.

Out of the offering of the believer's total self to God will come a *developing* discipline. The change in tense as we move from verse 1 to verse 2 is significant. The flavor of the tense in verse 1 suggests a decisive act; a specific and particular response of the believer to God's great mercies. When we come to verse 2 it is no longer a decisive act, but rather an ongoing experience as all three verb forms are now in the present tense. It is now a matter of daily resisting being conformed to the pattern of this world as a matter of lifestyle while continually and increasingly being transformed by the renewing of our mind.

The word "world" could better be translated "age." Although this world is given to the believer to enjoy, Satan is the God of this age. He seeks to woo the believer's affection away from his God. It is the spirit of this age that we are to resist. The transformed mind recognizes that this world is not all there is; rather, it is only the preface to a richer life to come. The transformed mind resists the impulse to get all one can now and seeks to store up treasures where moth and rust do not corrupt. Rather than build the world around one's ego, the transformed mind makes Christ the center of his life. The spirit of this age says, "What is mine is mine, and I'll keep it," or even more crassly, "What is yours is mine. If I can get it I'll take it." The transformed mind is the mind of Christ, which says, "What is mine is yours. I'll give it for the glory of God."

The final issue of this kind of movement from self toward God is that the believer finds a *daily dynamic* in being able to "prove what the will of God is." Clearly, what God wants for His child is always good and pleasing and perfect. How could our great God want anything less for His children? The problem comes in our being able to discover in concrete terms and circumstances what, in fact, is that will of God. As the verb indicates, that discovery is not always easy. There is no magic formula. Here, as elsewhere, easy answers are misleading. Rather, it is a matter of continual testing and probing through appropriating the mind of Christ (by His Word and by prayer) that we can "prove" without fear or hesitation that we are walking each day in the will of God.

What God wants from us is *always* God's best for us!

Think Straight About Your Gifts
(Romans 12:3-8)

Few subjects have been more warmly debated within the Christian community in recent years than that of spiritual gifts. In introducing this subject the apostle Paul says, "Think straight!" He purposefully uses language in a beautiful way to play on words in Romans 12:3. Not apparent in our translations, literally it is, "*Don't think grandly beyond what you ought to think, but think so as to think straight.*"

Many Christians today very boldly say, "*That* can't be a gift from God." Others with equal boldness affirm, "Look at my gift, it is better than yours." Some may even say, "Unless you have my gift, you're not in God's family at all!"

What do we see when we think straight?

First, *every believer has a gift.* Perhaps he has more than one gift, or even a rich variety of gifts. Paul's manner of address is very personal. "I say to every man among you" (v. 3). He emphasizes this again in verse 5 where he says, "we, who are many, are one body" and even more clearly in verse 6, "We have gifts that differ." So don't look down on your brothers and sisters—they have gifts, too! And, remember, they are differing gifts.

Thinking straight on this issue will provide a needed corrective for those of the Lord's people who think less of themselves than they should. Don't look down on yourself, for you are gifted. Nobody has been left out. Paul says in his first letter to the Corinthians that the Spirit distributes to each believer individually (12:11).

Each gift is important, for the sovereign Lord of the church would not distribute gifts of little or no importance to His children.

The word "gift" comes from the same root as the word "grace." Since grace is unmerited favor, our spiritual gifts are also an unmerited favor. The Spirit distributes as *He* wills.

Who are you? You are the recipient of God's gracious gift(s). Those who might think of themselves more highly than they ought to think should remember that the gift(s) they have are not because of their efforts, but because of His grace.

When we think straight on this subject we come to understand that *gifts are to be shared* with others. Our text makes it very clear that gifts are not given only to enrich the individual who receives the gift(s), but rather that through the exercise of gifts the entire body might be blessed. "We . . . are . . . individually members of one another" (v. 5).

There are priorities among gifts. If that were not so, how could Paul write to the Corinthians admonishing them to "desire the greater gifts?" If there are better or greater gifts, there must also be lesser gifts. How do we know which are which?

When we study carefully the classic passage on spiritual gifts in 1 Corinthians 12-14 it soon becomes apparent that the gifts that are more exotic or "showy" are to be evaluated in relation to their teaching function. It is interesting to note that in Romans, which is the most profound and theological of his epistles, Paul does not even mention those exotic gifts; miracles, tongues, and interpretation of tongues.

Instead, there are seven gifts listed, and every one of the seven finds its expression in reaching out to others. Of the seven in our list, three are gifts of instruction and proclamation whereas the rest relate to service to others.

As in the longer discussion in 1 Corinthians, Paul makes it very clear that the teaching gifts are the better gifts. If one is to seek a gift, that is the kind of gift to desire.

Gifts in general are to be evaluated in relation to their instructional content. First on the list is prophecy, which means to announce the will and intent of almighty God (*forth*telling—not making predictions). The content in teaching is clearly emphasized by the phrase, "according to the proportion of his faith" (v. 6). It is important to note that "his" in our translation represents the definite article in the Greek text. The literal translation would be "according to *the* faith"—the objective system of doctrine that stands as the basis of our faith. The text then carries the same thrust as in James: "the faith once for all delivered to the saints."

In addition to prophesying, there are the gifts of "teaching" and the more specialized "exhortation." "Exhortation" adds a note of urgency to the instruction.

Three of the seven gifts have instructional value. The remaining four; serving, contributing to the needs of others, leadership, and showing mercy are all gifts that relate to the corporate body of believers. Not a single gift can be exercised in isolation with a focus on one's own need and circumstances. Serving obviously requires someone to serve. Contributing to the needs of others specifically challenges us to forget ourselves. The gift of leadership cannot be exercised apart from brothers and sisters to be led. Showing mercy demands an object to receive that mercy.

To think as straight as we ought in the matter of spiritual gifts requires that we see the importance of every God-given gift. But we are to recognize that the instructional gifts have priority, as those gifts nourish and regulate the other gifts.

Gifts are to be used. Note the repeated phrase, "let each exercise." Let him teach. Let him encourage. Use your gift. The whole Body will suffer if you do not. Even more serious a matter, if you do not use your gift, your Lord will be deprived of glory that is rightfully His!

Remember Paul's caution not to think too highly of yourself—but don't put yourself down, either!

LISTEN TO WHAT THESE NOTARIZED WITNESSES SAY! (Romans 2:15; 8:16; 9:1)

How do you know when a statement is true? What kind of testimony does it take to convince you? A principle demonstrated repeatedly in the Bible is that to attest that a story is true requires not only a trustworthy witness, but also a corroborating witness. That is the basis for our modern legal system, which acquits or convicts according to what kind of witness has been established.

More than once some very wild-sounding rumors have first begun to gain credibility when more than one witness was found. The domino effect of corroborating witnesses has led to the downfall of many powerful men.

A compound verb, "summartureō" (literally meaning "to bear witness along with"), occurs three times in this epistle and nowhere else in the New Testament. Since Romans is rich in legal overtones, these occurrences should cause us to take special notice.

Just who or what are those witnesses, and to what irrefutable truths do they testify?

Man's conscience is a witness agreeing with natural revelation (Rom. 2:15). "They show the work of the Law written in their hearts, their conscience [also] bearing witness, and their thoughts alternately accusing or else defending them." Though "also" does not appear in the Greek text, it reflects the scope of this compound verb. Man's conscience bears witness along with something or someone else. What is that?

The context leaves no room for doubt. Paul has been arguing that natural man is without excuse, that quite apart from the gospel the natural man is utterly guilty before God because God has revealed himself in *nature*. When man does not live up to that light, he shamefully ignores the witness of creation to the majesty and power of God.

Paul indicts man further as he points out that man's conscience agrees with the witness of the natural creation, and he adds an intriguing expansion: "their thoughts alternately accusing or else defending them."

The text suggests clearly that man's conscience may defend him, that is, it may witness in his favor because he has acted upon the witness of natural creation, which tells him that God is real and true. Occasionally we hear of a pagan tribe's just waiting to receive the gospel from a missionary because they have not rejected the testimony of their consciences (however hazy or dim), but have seen God in creation and know that He must be the true and living God.

Man's conscience may defend him, but that is exceedingly rare. Ordinarily, man's conscience will accuse rather than defend. Conscience will accuse the heathen and testify to their guilt in failing to respond to the light they have. Conscience will accuse the more sophisticatedly enlightened many times over for their flagrant rejection of greater light. Conscience will most strongly accuse those who have heard the gospel for turning away not only from the testimony of nature but from the clear word of the gospel message.

Just as man's conscience testifies to his guilt before God, a witness of condemnation, there is a wonderful witness of justification. *The*

Holy Spirit is a witness agreeing with the believer's spirit. "The Spirit Himself bears witness with our spirit that we are the children of God" (Rom. 8:16). The first witness was bad news. This witness is good news—the very best of news. The bad news imputes guilt; the good news imputes righteousness.

It is a wonderful thing to have the full assurance of salvation, with our spirits' not condemning us but rather affirming that we are indeed the children of God. But the human spirit is frail. It has a tendency to doubt itself, and it is an unreliable witness because it could be in error. We stand in need of further assurance and affirmation by an entirely trustworthy corroborating witness.

The child of God has a much greater witness than his own spirit. "The Spirit *Himself* bears witness with our spirit." "Spirit" has a capital S, which speaks now of the Holy Spirit of God Himself, a greater witness of utmost dignity and impeccable integrity.

Several times in other letters Paul speaks of the believer's having been "sealed" by the Holy Spirit. What is that seal? Although it may involve more than this, it is the irrevocable confirmation whereby the Spirit of God goes on record to guarantee both to us and to God that we are indeed the children of God.

Paul's final witness is highly individualized and personal. An *awakened conscience* is a witness agreeing with natural inclination (9:1). "I am telling the truth in Christ, I am not lying, my conscience bearing me witness in the Holy Spirit, that I have great sorrow and unceasing grief in my heart. For I could wish that I myself were accursed, separated from Christ for the sake of my brethren . . . who are Israelites" (vv. 1-4). This is a cry of deep pathos and almost unfathomable intensity of desire, but it is also a cry of integrity as Paul calls almighty God to witness the depth of his desire for the people of Israel. Since Paul was a Jew ("my kinsmen") and since Paul well knew the rich heritage of his people (the adoption as sons, the divine glory, the covenants, the receiving of the law, the Temple worship, the promises, the patriarchs from whom is traced the human ancestry of Christ), all his human instincts fed his deep concern for his people.

We must see that that was more than mere human, prejudicial concern. His was a desire that anguished out of his conscience—a Holy Spirit-informed conscience. "My conscience bearing me witness in the Holy Spirit," Paul says (v. 1). That enlightened conscience, along with all of his natural pulls, converged into an intense desire to see his people saved or attain righteousness.

Too easily we assume so little responsibility or caring for the eternal destiny of those around us. Is that because we have not allowed the Holy Spirit to awaken our consciences as Paul had? Have we grieved the Spirit through disobedience to the point of a dulled conscience?

As man's conscience unites with natural revelation to witness to man's sin, and the Holy Spirit unites with the believer's spirit to witness to his salvation, so the Holy Spirit-informed conscience ought to unite with the believer's personal desire for family and friends to become members of the family of God.

What excuse can there be for not sharing the good news, the gospel, with those who are dearest and nearest?

WHAT DOES IT TAKE TO BE A "SUPER SAINT"?
(Romans 5:20; 8:26, 37; 12:3)

In recent years "super" has become one of society's "in" words. Used as an adjective it denotes the very best, the most, and the ultimate. So there is superman, superwoman, super hot dogs, super-suds, and so on. When used alone, "super" seems to be the most enthusiastic response one can give.

In the Greek language of the New Testament there is an interesting preposition which when prefixed by the letter "s" is pronounced like our English "super" and has much the same meaning. The word appears a number of times in Romans, but only four times is it prefixed to a verb to form a compound verb. Each of those four verbs is distinctive in that its occurrence in Romans is the only time it is used at all in the New Testament, and in each of the four cases a contrast is being made.

The first of the four speaks of *super-grace* (Rom. 5:20). "The Law came in that the transgression might increase; but where sin increased, *grace abounded all the more*, that, as sin reigned in death, even so grace might reign through righteousness to eternal life through Jesus Christ our Lord." Literally, "where sin increased, grace super-increased."

There is contrast here in the way the coming of the law put the focus on man's sin to make sin a visible, heinous thing that cannot be ignored or evaded. The last half of verse 20 is a purpose clause. The law was added for the very purpose and intent that sin might "stick out." The purpose of God's law was to make it very apparent what sin is so that it can be seen in all its horror to "increase" our awareness and estimation of its awfulness.

But now, wonder of wonders, *where* (in the very same arena) sin increased, grace super-increased. That takes us back to verses 18 and 19. Sin entered the world through the transgression of one man (Adam). By his unrighteous act all became sinners. In the same way, grace entered the world through one man (Jesus), and by His one righteous act (taking upon Himself our sin) any man who believes is declared righteous by a holy God. That is super-grace!

Sin that entered the world through Adam was made more apparent or shown for what it really is when the law was given. Grace, too, had been a reality from the beginning, but the gracious character of God was made clear and visible when Jesus perfectly fulfilled all the demands of that law in offering Himself as a sacrifice for the sinner's transgression of that law. That is God's grace super-abounding!

The second verb refers to *super-prayer*. "In the same way the Spirit also helps us in our weakness; for we do not know how to pray as we should, but the Spirit Himself intercedes for us with groanings too deep for words" (Rom. 8:26).

Unfortunately, the strong and vivid compound word is here translated by "intercedes." "*Super*-intercedes" literally makes the point.

Here again the contrast is clear. It is between our feeble ability to pray and the Holy Spirit's unlimited access to the Father. It is between our weakness and His strength. It is between our limited knowledge in not knowing what to pray for and His omniscience as the third person in the Godhead who knows all things. It is between our misdirected praying in failing to understand God's will and His intercession for us that is unfailingly "according to the will of God" (v. 27).

To the believer who will receive it the Holy Spirit offers "super-praying" in his behalf!

The third compound verb speaks of *super-triumph* and appears in Romans 8:37 in one of the most powerful statements of Christian victory in the entire Bible. "In all these things we overwhelmingly conquer through Him who loved us." Literally, we "super-conquer" through Jesus Christ!

To catch the power and majesty of the concept we need to look at the preceding words. "*In all these things* we overwhelmingly conqueror." In what things? We must go back to the things listed in verse 35: trouble, hardship, persecution, famine, nakedness, danger, and the sword. The notion that only men of faith can handle those things simply will not hold water. A good man in his own strength may be able to grit his teeth and conquer even in very trying situations.

But herein is the glorious contrast! Through our Lord who loves us we have infinite resources available not only to "super-conquer" in the end, but to "super-triumph" in the midst of pain and trial!

The last "super" is a prohibition. *Don't super-rate yourself!* "Do not think of yourself more highly than you ought, but rather think of yourself with sober judgment, in accordance with the measure of faith God has given you." (Rom. 12:3). Do not "super-think" of yourself or "super-evaluate" yourself!

In the light of all the blessings of grace that super-abounds, the help of the Spirit who super-prays for us, and the super-conquering available through Christ, the believer might easily be tempted to overrate his capacities and glory in ways that are not appropriate. Paul warns strongly against becoming bigheaded or boastful.

Instead, the believer is to be very mindful that he has nothing except what he has received by grace; that all his blessings are by God's favor and are quite divorced from any merit on his part.

Here, too, is contrast. When the believer notes that the standard for conduct is "in accordance with the measure of faith" (v. 3), he sees how far short he comes and he will want to be super-cautious in evaluating himself.

Don't be humble and proud of it.

Don't be proud and act humble.

Do be a "super-saint" by super-grace, super-prayer, and super-triumph through faith in Jesus Christ!

WHAT MAKES A STRONG CHRISTIAN?
(Romans 14)

Most Christians would wish to be known as strong Christians and would be quick to take offense at any inference that they fit the "weaker brother" category. Yet, when the test comes, very frequently those we have judged as weak turn out to be strong and those we have looked upon as strong prove to be weak. What are the qualities of a strong Christian?

The apostle Paul sets out some guidelines in Romans 14. He gives three positive/negative couplets that are not only descriptive of the strong Christian, but also prescriptive as to how to help a weak Christian to become strong.

Don't condemn—do accept. The strong Christian does not condemn or even judge those Christians who disagree with him. Note how frequently Paul speaks of this:

> "Accept the one who is weak in faith, but not for the purpose of passing judgment on his opinions" (v. 1)

"Let not him . . . regard with contempt him"; "let not him . . . judge him"; "for God has accepted him" (v. 3)

"Who are you to judge. . . ? "He who eats, . . . and he who eats not, . . . does so for the Lord" (vv. 4, 6)

"Why do you *judge* your brother?" "For we will all stand before God's judgment" (v. 10)

"Let us not judge" (v. 13); "each of us will give an account for himself" (v. 12).

All of the above italicized words translate the same verb in the Greek text. The implied command in all of this is to accept a brother for what he is without judging him. He must follow his own conscience (v. 22).

While the strong Christian does not judge others, note the parameters specified: "on *disputable* matters" (v. 1). There are, we must recognize, those matters of right or wrong that are *not* subject to dispute and must be judged for what they are—good or evil. Since God has given us a revealed law and standard of morals, there are divine imperatives and moral absolutes that simply cannot be flouted with impunity. In those areas it is, in fact, our Christian duty to speak unequivocably of God's standard as declared in His Word and to warn the transgressors.

However, when it comes to matters of individual preference or conscience, Paul says that in those areas we are not to judge, but rather we are to accept one another in Christ without criticism even though life-styles and practice may differ. The key is found in verse 1. There is an ambiguity, perhaps even a deliberate double meaning in the Greek text. We could translate it as the NASB does, "accept the one who is weak in faith." We could also translate with equal validity, "in faith accept the one who is weak." Our ability to accept the weaker brother thus becomes a measure of our faith!

The one whose faith is weak needs to be lovingly accepted without judgment even though we may not agree with him on secondary matters. Two very terse statements pull together the thrust of this passage: "Therefore, let us stop passing judgment on one another" (v. 13); "so whatever you believe about these things *keep between yourself and God*" (v. 22).

Don't offend—do edify. Following the apostle's exhortation to cease and desist passing judgment on one another, Paul tells what we should do. "But rather determine this—not to put an obstacle or a stumbling block in a brother's way. . . . So then let us pursue the things which make for peace and the building up of one another" (vv. 13, 19).

It is interesting to note that in verse 13 we have the same word translated "make up your mind" which in verses 1, 3-4, 10, 12-13 is translated "judge" or "condemn." There is one clear, strong judgment Paul would have us make: We will not offend a fellow Christian!

Paul goes on to give us some very strong medicine. He says that the believer should be willing to abstain from even the most innocent of activities if that activity offends a weaker brother. The response of a weak Christian to this strong medicine will no doubt be, "In Christ I am free to do my own thing." One must be strong in order to "bear the failings of the weak" when that means foregoing innocent pleasures or even abstaining from food.

But that is not all. We must not offend or tear down, but we must go beyond that to edify or build up. We cannot settle for a halfhearted or casual commitment. Rather, we must "pursue the things which make for peace and the building up of one another" (v. 19). The verb is a strong one. We are to pursue with great vigor the ministry of building up one another.

Don't serve self—do serve Christ. Underlying the whole chapter is the reality that each individual believer, be he weak or strong, is his Lord's servant. The servant or slave has one responsibility—to serve his Lord. He answers to his Lord and to no one else. What makes judging our brother deadly is that we put ourselves in Christ's place and ask our brother to serve us! Hence, judging our brother is indeed self-serving. When we accept our weaker brother and build him up, we serve the Lord. We help our brother to become a more profitable servant to our Lord, to whom alone he is responsible.

Weak Christians serve themselves, impose their standards on others, judge and condemn one another, and so weaken the Body of Christ.

Strong Christians serve the Lord, carefully consider the stand of fellow Christians with whom they disagree, love and build up one another, and so strengthen the Body of Christ.

How you treat a "weaker in faith" Christian is, indeed, a measure of your faith!

NOTE

1. Donald Grey Barnhouse, *Romans* (Grand Rapids: Eerdmans, 1952), 1:3.

Appendix

THE RELATIONSHIP BETWEEN THE BOOKS OF THE NEW TESTAMENT

Book	Date	Author	Pivotal Verses	Pivotal Words	Possible Themes
Matthew	A.D. 65	Matthew	27:37	kingdom of Heaven, fulfilled, Son of David	The gospel of the kingdom; Jesus the King
Mark	A.D. 59	John Mark	2:10; 10:45	straightway, Kingdom of God, immediately, service	Jesus, the Servant
Luke	A.D. 61	Luke	1:14; 19:10	Son of Man, Jesus	Jesus, the Man
John	A.D. 90	John	20:30-31	life, believe	Jesus, the Son of God
Acts	A.D. 61	Luke	1:8	witness, power, Holy Spirit	The development of Christianity under the Holy Spirit
Romans	A.D. 55	Paul	1:16-17	salvation, righteousness	Justification by faith: its method and result
1 Corinthians	A.D. 54	Paul	1:2-3; 2:7-8	grace, wisdom	Christian conduct
2 Corinthians	A.D. 55	Paul	7:6-7; 12:9	comfort, ministry	The greatest apostle of the Christian church

Galatians	A.D. 48	Paul	2:20; 3:2;5:1	faith, law, grace	Christ: The Deliverer from the law
Ephesians	A.D. 60	Paul	1:3; 3:19; 4:13	in Christ, all, fulness, church	The Church: the Body of Christ
Philippians	A.D. 61	Paul	4:4;1:21; 3:7, 14	gain, rejoice	Rejoice in the Lord
Colossians	A.D. 60	Paul	2:10 3:3	complete, Christ, Lord	the preeminent Christ
1 Thessalonians	A.D. 51	Paul	1:10; 5:16-18	brethren, Christ, Lord	The second coming of the Lord.
2 Thessalonians	A.D. 51	Paul	3:5	Christ	The second coming of the Lord
1 Timothy	A.D. 62	Paul	1:15; 3:9	command, teach doctrine, good works, godliness	The pastor's charge
2 Timothy	A.D. 63	Paul	1:13; 4:7-8	ashamed, endure	The necessity for straight living
Titus	A.D. 62	Paul	2:10; 3:8-9	sound, adorn, profitable, sober, good works	Encourage belief in and practice of sound doctrine
Philemon	A.D. 60	Paul	9, 17	receive, love	Christian servitude— the practice of Christian forgiveness
Hebrews	A.D. 64	Uncertain from evidence	11:40	better, Son, covenant	Jesus: High Priest & mediator of N.T.
James	A.D. 45	James, brother of Jesus	1:22; 2:26	brethren, faith, doer, works, wisdom	The practice of faith

1 Peter	A.D. 62	Peter	2:16-17	precious, suffering, behavior	Victory over suffering
2 Peter	A.D. 63	Peter	1:21	remembrance	Steadfastness until judgment
1 John	A.D. 90	John	3:1; 5:13	know, love, fellowship, flesh	The divine family; Jesus the Son of God; the letter of love
2 John	A.D. 90	John	6	truth, walk	The value of doctrine
3 John	A.D. 90	John	8	truth, fellow helper	Christian hospitality
Jude	A.D. 63	Jude	3, 21, 24-25	keep, kept	Constancy amid corruption
Revelation	A.D. 95	John	1:1, 19	Revelation, seven, Lamb	Jesus, the Lamb of God

Appendix 2

By answering the following questions, you may see how much you have grasped.

TRUE OR FALSE:

1. There were more Jews than Gentiles in Rome at the time of this epistle. _____
2. Romans was written during Paul's second missionary journey. _____
3. "Heaven" and "hell" are discussed extensively in Romans. _____
4. The words "righteousness" and "justification" come from the same root word. _____
5. The word "devil" does not occur in this epistle. _____
6. There are twenty-six salutations in Romans. _____
7. We learn little about the church at Rome in Romans. _____
8. Romans is one of nine church epistles. _____
9. There are more references to "law" in the book of Romans than there are to "sin." _____
10. The doctrine of "grace" is concentrated almost entirely in chapters 1-3. _____
11. Romans 1:1-7 is composed of one sentence. _____

FILL IN THE BLANK:

12. God is revealed through the gospel, _____ , conscience, and through Christ.
13. In what two chapters would you find the "evidences" of the Christian life? _____ and _____ .
14. Romans was written from the city of _____ .
15. If repentance means a change of mind, _____ means a change of direction.
16. The practice of righteousness in civil duties is discussed in chapter _____ .

17. The prison epistles of Paul were written in A.D. 62. They are letters to the _____ , _____ , _____ , and to _____ .

18. Christian liberty in the areas of food and special days is discussed in chapter _____ .

19. Squaring the books with God is discussed in Romans ___ : ___ .

20. Romans 1:16 through 3:20 could be studied as a _____ scene.

LOCATE BY CHAPTER:

21. The wise use of gifts.   _____
22. Three great confessions.   _____
23. No condemnation, no obligation, and no separation.   _____
24. Debts paid and unpaid.   _____
25. They changed the truth of God into a lie.   _____
26. The Christian as his brother's keeper.   _____
27. The necessity, object, and outcome of faith.   _____
28. "Know," "reckon," and "yield."   _____
29. Christian liberty and Christian charity.   _____
30. The ground of justification is God's grace.   _____
31. Subjection to authority.   _____
32. "Of God" occurs fives times within four verses.   _____
33. "Glory" or "boast" occurs three times.   _____
34. Deliverance from indwelling sin.   _____
35. Principles of judgment.   _____
36. The sovereignty of God.   _____
37. The reason, remedy, and result of Israel's rejection.   _____
38. "For the wrath of God is revealed . . . against all
    ungodliness . . . of men, who suppress the truth."   _____
39. Justified by grace, blood, and faith.   _____
40. There are three deaths referred to in Romans:
    death to sin   _____
    death to the law   _____
    death to the flesh.   _____
41. The assurance, endurance, confirmation, and
    consummation of hope.   _____
42. Union with Christ in the body.   _____
43. The power of holiness.   _____
44. The doctrine of election is emphasized.   _____
45. Servant, Son, and saints.   _____
46. Righteousness offered to all, on faith, freely by grace.   _____

MISCELLANEOUS QUESTIONS:

47. Locate the three doxologies in the book of Romans:
    ___ : _____ ; ___ : _____ ; ___ : _____ .

48. What significance does Job 9:2 have in the study of the contents of the book of Romans? _____
    _____ .

49. "The just shall live by faith" is found in Habakkuk 2:4; Hebrews 10:38; Galatians 3:11; and Romans ___ : ___ .

50. Arrange the following doctrines from 1 to 6 in order of frequency of reference: grace, sin, law, Jesus Christ, Holy Spirit, and righteousness.

    1. _____   4. _____
    2. _____   5. _____
    3. _____   6. _____ .

51. Romans is a book of logic. Locate by chapter the following "therefore's."
    The "therefore" of condemnation _____
    The "therefore" of justification _____
    The "therefore" of no condemnation _____
    The "therefore" of dedication _____ .

52. Seven words in Romans 1:16-17 give seven prominent themes in the book of Romans: _____ , _____ , _____ ,
    _____ , _____ , _____ , and
    _____ .

GIVE THE MEANING:

53. "Saints" _____ .
54. "Jesus" _____ .
55. "Gospel" _____ .
56. "Grace" _____ .
57. "To sanctify" _____ .
58. "Servant" (in Rom. 6) _____ .

Appendix 3

Here are the answers to the review questions.

TRUE OR FALSE:

1. There were more Jews than Gentiles in Rome at the
   time of this epistle.   F

2. Romans was written during Paul's second missionary
   Journey.   F (3rd)

3. "Heaven" and "hell" are discussed extensively in
   Romans.   F

4. The words "righteousness" and "justification" come
   from the same root word.   T

5. The word "devil" does not occur in this epistle.   T

6. There are twenty-six salutations in Romans.   T

7. We learn little about the church at Rome in Romans.   T

8. Romans is one of nine church epistles.   T

9. There are more references to "law" in the book of
   Romans than there are to "sin."   T

10. The doctrine of "grace" is concentrated almost entirely
    in chapters 1-3.   F

11. Romans 1:1-7 is composed of one sentence.   T

FILL IN THE BLANK:

12. God is revealed through the gospel, __nature__ , conscience, and
    through Christ.

13. In what two chapters would you find the "evidences" of the Christian life? __12__ and __13__ .

14. Romans was written from the city of __Corinth__ .

15. If repentance means a change of mind, __conversion__ means
    a change of direction.

16. The practice of righteousness in civil duties is discussed in chapter __13__ .

17. The prison epistles of Paul were written in A.D. 62. They are letters to the ___Philippians___ , ___Colossians___ , ___Ephesians___ , and to ___Philemon___ .
18. Christian liberty in the areas of food and special days is discussed in chapter ___14___ .
19. Squaring the books with God is discussed in Romans _14_ : _12_ .
20. Romans 1:16 through 3:20 could be studied as a ___court___ scene.

LOCATE BY CHAPTER:

21. The wise use of gifts.   _12_
22. Three great confessions.   _7_
23. No condemnation, no obligation, and no separation.   _8_
24. Debts paid and unpaid.   _13_
25. They changed the truth of God into a lie.   _1_
26. The Christian as his brother's keeper.   _14_
27. The necessity, object, and outcome of faith.   _4_
28. "Know," "reckon," and "yield."   _6_
29. Christian liberty and Christian charity.   _14_
30. The ground of justification is God's grace.   _3_
31. Subjection to authority.   _13_
32. "Of God" occurs fives times within four verses.   _13_
33. "Glory" or "boast" occurs three times.   _5_
34. Deliverance from indwelling sin.   _6_
35. Principles of judgment.   _2_
36. The sovereignty of God.   _9_
37. The reason, remedy, and result of Israel's rejection.   _10_
38. "For the wrath of God is revealed . . . against all ungodliness . . . of men, who suppress the truth."   _1_
39. Justified by grace, blood, and faith.   _3_
40. There are three deaths referred to in Romans:
    death to sin   _6_
    death to the law   _7_
    death to the flesh.   _8_
41. The assurance, endurance, confirmation, and consummation of hope.   _5_
42. Union with Christ in the body.   _6_
43. The power of holiness.   _8_
44. The doctrine of election is emphasized.   _9_
45. Servant, Son, and saints.   _1_
46. Righteousness offered to all, on faith, freely by grace. _3_

MISCELLANEOUS QUESTIONS:

47. Locate the three doxologies in the book of Romans:
__8__ : __38-39__ ; __11__ : __33-36__ ; __16__ : __25-27__ .

48. What significance does Job 9:2 have in the study of the contents of
the book of Romans? ____How shall a man be justified with God?____

49. "The just shall live by faith" is found in Habakkuk 2:4; Hebrews
10:38; Galatians 3:11; and __1__ : __17__ .

50. Arrange the following doctrines from 1 to 6 in order of frequency
of reference: grace, sin, law, Jesus Christ, Holy Spirit, and righteousness.

1. ___law_____   4. ___righteousness_____
2. ___Christ_____   5. ___Holy Spirit_____
3. ___sin_____   6. ___grace_____ .

51. Romans is a book of logic. Locate by chapter the following
"therefore's."

The "therefore" of condemnation _____3_____
The "therefore" of justification _____5_____
The "therefore" of no condemnation _____8_____
The "therefore" of dedication _____12_____ .

52. Seven words in Romans 1:16-17 give seven prominent themes in
book of the Romans: ___God___ , ___gospel___ , ___faith___ ,
___power___ , ___salvation___ , ___life___ , and
___righteousness___ .

GIVE THE MEANING:

53. "Saints" _____holy ones_____ .
54. "Jesus" _____Savior-Joshua_____ .
55. "Gospel" _____good news_____ .
56. "Grace" _____unmerited favor_____ .
57. "To sanctify" _____to set apart_____ .
58. "Servant" (in Rom. 6) _____slave to righteousness_____ .

Bibliography

Ackroyd, P.R., ed. *The Letter of Paul to the Romans*. The Cambridge Bible Commentary on the New English Bible. Cambridge: Cambridge U., 1967.

Baillie, J.; McNeill, John T.; and Van Dusen, Henry P., eds. *Luther: Lectures on Romans*. The Library of Christian Classics, vol. 15. Translated by Wilhelm Pauck. Philadelphia: Westminster, 1961.

Barrett, C.K. *A Commentary on the Epistle to the Romans*. New York: Harper & Row, 1957.

Baxter, J. Sidlow. *Acts to Revelation*. Explore the Book, vol. 6. London: Marshall, Morgan & Scott, 1955.

————. *The Strategic Grasp of the Bible*. 7th ed. Grand Rapids: Zondervan, 1968.

Blass, F., and Debrunner, A. *A Greek Grammar of the New Testament and Other Early Christian Literature*. 5th ed. Translated and revised by Robert W. Funk. Chicago: U. of Chicago, 1961.

Bruce, F. F. *The Epistle of Paul to the Romans*. Tyndale New Testament Commentaries. 5th ed. Grand Rapids: Eerdmans, 1963.

Conybeare, W. J., and Howson, J. S. *The Life and Epistles of St. Paul*. Grand Rapids: Eerdmans, 1950.

Corley, Bruce, and Vaughan, Curtis. *Romans: A Study Guide Commentary*. Grand Rapids: Zondervan, 1976.

Cranfield, C. E. B. *Romans I–VIII*. A Critical and Exegetical Commentary on the Epistle to the Romans, vol. 1. Edinburgh: T. & T. Clark, 1975.

Danker, Frederick W. *Multipurpose Tools for Bible Study*. St. Louis: Concordia, 1960.

Dodd, C. H. *The Epistle of Paul to the Romans*. New York: Harper & Row, 1932.

Donfried, Karl P., ed. *The Romans Debate: Essays on the Origin & Purpose of the Epistle*. Minneapolis: Augsburg, 1977.

Evans, William. *Romans and First and Second Corinthians*. Through the Bible Book by Book. New York: Revell, 1918.

Ferrin, Howard W. *Outline Studies in the Book of Romans*. Providence, R.I.: Providence Bible Institute, 1941.

Gifford, E. H. *The Epistle of St. Paul to the Romans*. 1886. Reprint. Minneapolis: James Family, 1977.

Godet, F. Commentary of St. Paul's Epistle to the Romans. Translated by Rev. A. Cusin. Edinburgh: T. & T. Clark, 1886.

Gutzke, Manford G. Plain Talk on Romans. Grand Rapids: Zondervan, 1976.

Harrison, Norman B. His Salvation as Set Forth in the Book of Romans. 10th ed. Chicago: Moody, 1924.

Hayes, D. A. Paul and His Epistles. New York: Methodist Book Concern, 1915.

James, Edgar C. Romans: Amazing Grace! Chicago: Moody, 1973.

Kasemann, Ernst. Commentary on the Epistle to the Romans. Translated by Geoffrey W. Bromiley. Grand Rapids: Eerdmans, 1978.

Lange, John P. The Epistle of Paul to the Romans. Commentary on the Holy Scriptures, vol. 10. Translated by John Peter Lange. Grand Rapids: Zondervan, 1960.

Leenhardt, F. J. The Epistle to the Romans. Cleveland, Oh.: World, 1957.

Lenski, R. C. H. Interpretation of Romans. Minneapolis: Augsburg, 1961.

McClain, Alva J. Romans: The Gospel of God's Grace. Edited by Herman A. Hoyt. Chicago: Moody, 1973.

Mears, Henrietta. What the Bible is All About. 4th ed. Glendale, Calif.: Gospel Light, 1953.

Morgan, G. Campbell. Living Messages of the Books of the Bible: Old and New Testaments. Westwood, N.J.: Revell, 1912.

Murray, John. The Epistle to the Romans. 3rd ed. Grand Rapids: Eerdmans, 1968.

Newman, Barclay M., and Nida, Eugene A. A Translator's Handbook on Paul's Letter to the Romans. Helps for Translators, vol. 14. London: United Bible Societies, 1973.

Perry, Lloyd M., and Culver, Robert D. How to Search the Scriptures. Grand Rapids: Baker, 1967.

Price, Walter K. Revival in Romans. Grand Rapids: Zondervan, 1962.

Richards, Lawrence O. Creative Bible Study. Grand Rapids: Zondervan, 1971.

————. Creative Bible Teaching. Chicago: Moody, 1970.

Robertson, Archibald T. The Epistles of Paul. Word Pictures in the New Testament, vol. 4. Nashville: Broadman, 1930.

Sanday, William, and Headlam, Arthur C. Romans. International Critical Commentary Series. Greenwood, S. C.: Attic, 1977.

Scroggie, W. Graham. Know Your Bible. Old Tappan, N.J.: Revell, 1965.

Simeon, Charles. *Romans. Expository Outlines on the Whole Bible,* vol. 15. Grand Rapids: Zondervan, 1955.

Spence, H. D. M., and Exell, Joseph S., eds. *Acts and Romans.* The Pulpit Commentary, vol. 18. 3rd ed. Grand Rapids: Eerdmans, 1950.

Stalker, James. *The Life of St. Paul.* New York: American Tract Society, 1892.

Talbot, Louis T. *Addresses on Romans.* 2nd ed. Wheaton Ill.: Van Kampen, 1936.

Tenney, Merrill C. *New Testament Survey.* Grand Rapids: Eerdmans, 1961.

Thomas, W. H. Griffith. *St. Paul's Epistle to the Romans.* 2nd ed. Grand Rapids: Eerdmans, 1946.

Walton, A. J. *Romans: Book of Power.* Nashville: Tidings, 1962.

Wiersbe, Warren W. *Be Right: An Expository Study of Romans.* 2nd ed. Wheaton, Ill.: Scripture Press, Victor, 1977.

Wuest, Kenneth S. *Romans in the Greek New Testament.* Grand Rapids: Eerdmans, 1955.